Living Together

BOOKS BY BARBARA B. HIRSCH

Divorce: What a Woman Needs to Know

Living Together: A Guide to the Law
for Unmarried Couples

Living Together

A Guide to the Law for Unmarried Couples

Barbara B. Hirsch

Houghton Mifflin Company Boston   1976

Library of Congress Cataloging in Publication Data

Hirsch, Barbara B
  Living together.

  Includes index.
  1. Unmarried couples — Legal status, laws, etc.
— United States. I. Title.
KF538.H57   346'.73'016   76-25987
ISBN 0-395-24780-2
ISBN 0-395-24977-5 *pbk*.

To my mother and father

ACKNOWLEDGMENTS

ALTHOUGH I have done my best to delete the "to wit"s, *per stirpes,* compounded prepositions, and *scilicets,* this book is a law book. I offer no expertise as to why people are living together or what effect, if any, these arrangements have on society today or in the future. Those are subjects for the behavioral sciences.

This is a law book for single people living together today or considering it for tomorrow, or who are enjoying their experiment with this new status or suffering the residual effects of a relationship gone awry. Its purpose is to explain the law's impact on this new personal status. As this is a law text, it is based on existing statutes and actual cases.

My gratitude to law students Bonnie and Jim, who dug through the libraries helping me find the precedents, and to Eve and Judy, who not only typed the draft but loyally assured me that the manuscript was at least a shade more interesting than the wills, deeds, and pleadings that normally take up their efforts. And since this is a guide for real people with real legal problems, my thanks to those very real people who talked to me about what pleased them and concerned them about their lives together.

BARBARA B. HIRSCH

CONTENTS

Living Together

1. Marriage vs. Consortium

MARRIAGE IS basic to human behavior. Just about every type of organized society has some form of marriage: some ritual, religious or otherwise, some set of Emily Post rules for what to wear, where to seat the bride's family at the campfire, the mystique surrounding the wedding night, the honeymoon, anniversaries, and so on. And why not? Marriage has always represented the elemental family unit, the appropriate atmosphere for sex and the rearing of offspring. We often judge the level of civilization of a people by the degree of ritual, stability, and fidelity they achieve in marriage — monogamous marriage in particular.

How long has marriage constituted the heart of civilization? That's a question we can leave for the fundamentalists to fight out with the sociologists.

But today the status of monogamous marriage is changing — in many ways has already changed. And a lot of factors have contributed to this change. Women, long believed to be the prime movers for marriage (or so the mythology has it), have discovered that they are well able to make their way through life on their own. We even admit that women have the same sexual drives as men. And planned parenthood has become a reality. Lurking behind all of the mythology was the belief that a man and woman could love each other and tell the world they did by declaring that they were committed to each other, 'til death them do part.

I believe in marriage. I love the idea of two people being in love forever.

A few weeks ago I was having a Coke with Charlie, a client,

at a restaurant near his grocery store. One of his friends sat down with us after his tennis game. We got into a discussion of marriage, not anyone's in particular, but in the abstract. The tennis player was very profound on the subject and defended the status of marriage against my only half-sincere onslaught. He told us that marriage is a special status between man and woman, the highest possible relationship. It is telling the world in general and the people closest to you that "my commitment to this woman and her commitment to me have reached the highest level and we are husband and wife." It all sounded beautiful. The music of a thousand violins swelled in the background. It was everything my mother had promised marriage would be. And then Charlie interrupted:

"So you're going to marry this one."

"Yeah."

"Now how many times have you been married?"

"Four or five."

And he finished off his Coke, picked up his tennis racket, and was gone.

Is that marriage? Is it a succession of "commitments"? If that's it — well, maybe the kids are right. Maybe there is an alternative and maybe that alternative provides the best of marriage, the bonuses, without the obligations and with a walk instead of a divorce court. Divorce has become so rampant, so common, so easy, so popular in fact, that marriage has lost the stamp of permanency. Children growing up in homes with one parent seem to be doing just fine.

Under the circumstances, it seems natural that people should change their attitudes towards the status of marriage. People used to be either married or single. If you were married, you bought a house, you had kids, filed joint tax returns, squeezed the same toothpaste tube, slept in the same bed, and vowed to stay together. If you were single, it was a negative situation: it meant that you had not managed to get married, and perhaps there was something wrong with you. Today, being single means that you've *opted* for this particular lifestyle. And now there is a third alternative: two single people who want to live together, somewhat married, but not.

This third alternative is, as I define it, a third option, a third *status*. I'm not talking about a casual weekend. I'm not describing a brief romantic interlude. I'm not talking about shacking up. No one has to write a book about that — it's fun or it's not. What this book explores is the substance of the commitment involved when two people love and honor each other and live together as if they were married, but are not. Whether you choose this status may be a matter so personal that no one can write a guidebook except for himself. But whether society allows the thriving of this third option, whether the law allows it to exist, is a matter of fact that deserves attention.

So let's take a little tour through the law and see what happens when single people live together — to them, to their children, to the Internal Revenue Service. Can they own property? Should they? Can they leave their insurance for each other? Can they lose their jobs and their cash? I can't advise you how to explain the new relationship to your family. But I have gone through the law books, and the purpose here is to explore the legal implications of this new relationship.

First, let's get a few things straight. This third alternative we are discussing is *not* marriage. It's not common-law marriage either.

Marriage is the lawful union of man and woman by ceremony, which joins the parties in a relationship that may be severed only by death or divorce.

Common-law marriage is the lawful union of man and woman by declaration, intention, and conduct, which in certain domiciliary states joins the parties in a relationship that may be severed only by death or divorce.

In most states of the United States, marriage is performed by ceremony — that is, a third person, authorized to perform marriages, conducts a ritual and joins the parties in lawful wedlock.

At last count eighteen states retain some form of common-law marriage.* Common-law marriage is the *same* as any other marriage but doesn't require a third person's saying the words to make it so. If a person is domiciled in a state which recognizes common-law marriage, he can be married by living with a person of the opposite sex, declaring that person to be his spouse. Both parties must actually intend their relationship to be a marriage. They are Mr. and Mrs. They may file joint tax returns and in all other respects conduct themselves as married people. Having established that relationship, they are married. If they live in a common-law state and that state is their home, then they are married wherever they travel and wherever they later reside. The only way to end a marriage, ceremonial or common-law, is by death or divorce. Annulment doesn't count because that is a legal procedure which declares null and void only a purported marriage which was, in fact, no marriage at all.

Marriage, whether ceremonial or common-law, includes with it all sorts of legal rights and duties. Marriage is a relationship which involves three parties: the husband, the wife, and the state. Severance of the relationship thus requires the intervention of the state, through its arm, the divorce court. To end a marriage the state has to intervene and declare the marriage ended and parcel out the rights and obligations. When the divorce judge places child custody in one spouse and visitation in the other, when he orders alimony, child support, a sale of some property, a division of other property, and so forth, he is acting for the state in wrapping up the marriage and settling all of these privileges and duties.

Single people living together, the third alternative, is neither ceremonial nor common-law marriage. It's a status arranged by the parties — without the state's approval when they commence the relationship and without the judge's intervention when they end it. The relationship, this commitment between

---

* Alabama, Colorado, Florida, Georgia, Idaho, Indiana, Iowa, Kansas, Michigan, Mississippi, Montana, Ohio, Oklahoma, Pennsylvania, Rhode Island, South Carolina, South Dakota, Texas.

two people to preserve single identities but to share their living and loving, is independent of the law and the state. This status doesn't even have a proper name.

At the prayer meeting they might call it "living in sin." Old-timers might call it "concubinage," but to the people who have opted for single-living-together status, these labels don't fit.

"I don't know what to call it." Jim was concerned. "There ought to be a title that describes how Carol and I live. We're not just shacking up."

That was apparent. Jim was sipping white wine from an Orrefors goblet in the living room of the high-rise apartment he and Carol have shared for a year or so. Nothing about their living together suggested "shacking up." Both he and Carol had been divorced and had opted for nonmarriage. But they seemed committed. Their apartment is put together with care that indicates permanence — or is it just that Jim is professionally a graphic designer and the apartment is an extension of his work with balance, light, and color. And was he truly committed to Carol or did she simply fit the style? Carol, in her mid-thirties, is fair and lean, with bony bare feet; she is wearing a cotton hostess dress patterned to pick up the contrasting fuchsias in the room. Is Carol as liberated and independent as she says she is? Will she roll her hair and put on her wrap-around housedress as soon as I leave and weep and wail and beg for Jim to marry her and make her an "honest" woman? I knew that wouldn't happen — and yet, what is their relationship?

"I can't call her my roommate — that's too cute," Jim went on. "I could call her my best friend, or my best friend whom I sleep with, but . . . I've thought of calling her 'my life' — I wouldn't call her 'my wife.' " He was emphatic.

Carol's marriage had lasted only a few years and there were no children. The divorce was traumatic emotionally but not legally. Jim's marriage had been long-term, involving three children and a house in the suburbs, and, when he left it, he was loaded with guilt, recriminations, and divorce settlements. But he's a new man now, he tells people. He's left the Scott's-Turf-

Builder-and-commuter-train existence for a life devoted to work (at which he is succeeding beyond any expectations he had when his life was split between office and suburbia), and he now has a personal relationship which leaves him feeling free and unencumbered yet committed and in love.

But what do we call this personal relationship? Would 7-Up be furious if I call it unmarriage? There are always the terms "lovers," "sweethearts," "loving," "commitment," but can't these fit married people too? Is it too cold to call this an arrangement, a partnership? My married, Catholic, straight, and straight-A law clerk combined the words "married" and "single" and suggested we call it "mingle." My response was to send him back to the law library to research the meaning of the good old reliable legal term "consortium."

Consortium means sex, services, and society, and a consort is one who provides them. Typically, the law speaks of consortium in terms of *unavailability* of sex, services, and society. For example, a man is injured in an automobile accident. He was innocently driving down the street, obeying the traffic ordinances and "in due care and caution for his own safety and the property of others." He was struck by a well-insured auto, driven by a well-insured motorist, in total disregard of the care of our man, and negligently, willfully, wantonly, and recklessly. Our guy is carried off to the hospital. While recovering in his neck brace, he is unable to perform on the job or at home. He sues — Count I to recover money for his injuries. She, his wife, sues — Count II for the loss of her husband's consortium caused by the negligent, willful, wanton, and reckless defendant.

Consortium, according to one appeals court, is material services, companionship, felicity, and sexual intercourse "all welded into a conceptualistic unity." According to another it is a "union or continuity of companionship" or "to keep company or to associate," and a consort is "a partner or colleague." The high courts of many states have defined consortium as fellowship and the right of each partner to "company, cooperation, affection, and aid."

"Consortium" has a nice ring. Business conglomerations call themselves consortiums to get away from the right word with the wrong implication: syndicate. I wonder if Jim and Carol would approve of the word "consortium" for their single-living-together and would call each other "consort" instead of roommate, concubine, lover, or worse, husband or wife. Consortium means the committed exchange of sex, services, and society. A consort is a male or female counterpart of that relationship.

Homosexuals have lived as consorts long before the single-living-together idea even occurred to heterosexual couples. Homosexuals who loved each other and sought permanency in their relationship had no alternative. They could not marry. As the gay liberation movement declares itself and makes us think, discriminatory law and conduct are diminishing. There even has been the case in which a state official has granted a marriage license to a homosexual couple. It makes the newspapers, but it is the *rare* case.

The 1970s and the new candor have brought forth a fresh area of legal contest in which the homosexual asserts his rights. Thus far it is not a success story. The usual case route for testing the rights of homosexuals to marry is the *mandamus* proceeding. *Mandamus* asks the court to *command* a governmental official to do his job. The job in question in the homosexual marriage cases is the issuance of a marriage license. In 1971, Richard and James, both adult males, applied for a marriage license and were refused. They brought a *mandamus* suit against the licensing clerk asking the court to *command* him to issue a license. First they argued that the marriage licensing statute made no reference to male or female. The judge disagreed, pointing to the "realistic" meaning of marriage from the state's "territorial days" and citing references to "husband and wife" and "bride and groom." Next the petitioners argued that it is unconstitutional to deny people the fundamental right to marry and that to do so is discriminatory. The court disagreed. It said that "the institution of marriage is a union of man and woman, uniquely involving the procreation and rearing of children within a family. It is as old as the book of Genesis." Richard and James argued that the state does not require heterosexual couples to prove their capacity or declare their willingness to procreate. True, said the judge, but nevertheless he refused them issuance of a marriage license.

In 1973, two women sought to have a marriage license issued. The judges refused them also, stating that marriage is a "legal union of a man with a woman" or "being united to a person of the opposite sex as husband and wife . . . for the purpose of founding and maintaining a family." The judges said that even if the women had concealed the fact that they were of the same sex and thus obtained a license and married, they still would not be legally married, for they "are prevented from marrying, not by the statutes . . . or the refusal of the County Court Clerk . . . to issue them a license, but rather by their own incapability of entering into a marriage as that term is defined." Still another case, in 1974, came to the same conclusion, even though the two male marriage-license applicants relied on the Equal Rights Amendment, which had passed their state. The amendment declares that "equality of rights and responsibility under the law shall not be denied or abridged on account of sex." The petitioners argued "to permit a man to marry a woman but at the same time to deny him the right to marry another man is to construct an unconstitutional classification 'on account of sex.' " Again the court refused to issue the marriage license, again stating that an attempted marriage between persons of the same sex is no marriage at all.

It is clear therefore that until the legislators and judges acknowledge that lawful marriage carries with it rights which should not be denied on the basis of sexuality, or homosexuality, consortium is the only relationship for homosexuals who seek a commitment.

Except for those sections clearly based on heterosexuality (abortion, for instance) the legal implications of consortium outlined in this book relate to homosexual as well as heterosexual consortium.

2. Bastards

OF ALL of the downtrodden, deprived, and underprivileged minorities, of all those who find themselves on the fringes of society, of all the debased, insulted, and ignored, there is none so barred from the acceptance of the community and protection of law as the bastard. The "illegitimate" doesn't even benefit from one redeeming stereotype which the bigot bestows on other minorities. He's neither sung about nor noted in legend. Rather, his name is on the lips of every waiter you don't tip and every cabdriver you cut off.

No doubt many couples who enter a "consortium" arrangement act on the principle that they will have no children. Whether they use condom, diaphragm, pill, vasectomy, or deep and abiding faith in sterility, old age, or luck, they assume there will be no children. But if we are really after a third option, if we want to dignify this relationship with honorable and permanent status, then it seems reasonable to include children in the concept of consortium.

The decision to have children or the decision forced upon you by unwanted pregnancy — whether to abort it or adopt the child out — deserves the greatest care. I suspect that single couples think about it a lot more than married couples. Single couples, while they deny it, assume change, break-up, "freedom." Married couples often admit to a longing for change, break-up, "freedom"; but in a romantic haze, assuming — against growing odds — the permanency of their relationship, and with a belief in the existence of legal protection for their offspring, they embark upon parentage as a natural progression — going steady, engagement, marriage, parenthood, death, and taxes. Historically, heterosexual monogamous marriage has been the protected relationship. Sociologists told us that other relationships were contrary to the preservation of society, the reproduction of the species being the raison d'être of life. But today, with hunger, pollution, and overpopulation becoming a growing concern, for many, childless consortium may be the answer. Certainly, many unmarried couples express dismay when asked whether their committed, loving relationship would produce offspring. Couple after couple said that if they decided to have children, they'd opt for traditional marriage. Why? The "bastard" stigma could fade away just as the stigma against the unmarried woman and man who live together is fading, but the couples I spoke to clung to the stigma as a reason (or an excuse?) for not having children. There is a tendency for the law to catch up with society and even, sometimes, lead society. If the law isn't helping the bastard, maybe it's because the committed consorts are using the present state of the law as a justification for remaining childless.

Let's assume that your consortium, or at least one of you, has the urge to have a baby. If you want a baby, at least one of you must be prepared to stick with the job for about twenty years, and that's a long term by anyone's count. Even assuming a normal, healthy, bright, and pretty baby, the primary issue for you both is that of commitment to get the job done.

A combination of biology and sexual roles may lead you men to assume that *she* will take care of your child, and she'll do it alone if you lose interest. If that's what's lurking behind your impulse to have a baby now, consider that you are bringing a real live person into this world. This is not the stamp collection, photography, or trombone-playing that was your passion, six months at a time, and then forgotten; this is not a hobby, fad, height of avant-garde, or the real shocker to your folks. This is a living human being you're talking about. You can't store the baby in a box in the attic when the thrill is gone.

A woman reading this is likely to be more aware of her role in bringing a bastard into the world. A woman knows that there will come a time when her slacks won't zip and her coat won't button. There is no way that a woman can keep her plans a secret from her grandmother or her boss. There is a whole raft of problems relating to her employment (so many, in fact, that I refer you to Chapter 11 on this subject). And, looking the statistics and realities squarely in the eye, the woman must be prepared to be the one who will carry this baby, not only until birth, but for many years afterward. If you are a woman, there is the inescapable possibility that you and the baby may be left on your own — such is the nature of the "free" relationship.

Weighing the joy of a baby against the duties and responsibilities of parenthood is the job of both of you. But before you make the decision, to have or not to have, you ought to know what you and the prospective child are in for as far as the law is concerned.

A whole body of law has developed around the questions of who is a bastard and how society treats him. His official title has been discussed in the legislatures and ruled upon by the courts. In some places, he's an "illegitimate," in others, a "child born out of wedlock." Elsewhere he may be considered a "bastard," or in some circles, a "love child" (implying, ironically, that every baby born of married couples is unloved).

A bastard is, of course, a child born out of wedlock. A child is not a bastard if he was conceived during a marriage that ended in divorce or annulment. So poor is the bastard's lot that legislatures have made a genuine effort to find legitimacy even if the strict interpretation of the law bends in the process. Assume, for example, that your mother and father married with the exchanging of blood tests and vows, and lived together until they died — along the line conceiving you and bringing you into the world. Your father dies a wealthy man, and at the funeral there arrive on the scene another woman and four offspring; it develops that she was your father's number 1 wife and never divorced. You are the child of a void marriage, but legitimate nevertheless. Or assume, if your delicate sensibilities and Oedipus complex allow, that your mother was not always faithful to her husband, your "father." You may be the only redhead in the family, but the presumption is that you're legit. Or, assume that your parents did what you're doing and conceived you prior to their legal marriage. After the official wedding, if Dad treats you as he treats your younger siblings, you're not a bastard either. Every so often, though, the law takes a step backwards and even the presumption of legitimacy has occasionally gone awry. Take, for example, the situation in which a judge held a child to be "born out of wedlock and therefore illegitimate," when it was conceived by artificial insemination of the sperm of an unidentified donor, with the consent of a lawfully married husband and wife.

Why this great concern over whether the child is legitimate or a bastard? Here we are in a liberalized society with the two of you living together, openly, notoriously, and who but Aunt Nellie gives a damn?

Your child might care. To be a bastard may be a social stigma that the child can't shake. Poor Alexander Hamilton, despite all his accomplishments, is still described in the texts as being of "uncertain descent." But this didn't stop Hamilton, so does it matter? It mattered to child Z, who sued his father for knowingly creating him a bastard. It seemed that his father seduced his mother with a promise of marriage when the cad knew all along that he was already married. When the child was born, a suit was brought by the baby to collect for the father's wrong of stigmatizing him a bastard. The judges accepted the premise that the kid was harmed and that it was tough to be a bastard, but they refused to order his father to reimburse him for his trauma, fearing that the "doors of litigation would be opened" to a "staggering" number of lawsuits — by bastards, and also by children born with hereditary diseases, children born into poverty, and children born with their mother's freckles. Baby W did no better in suing the whole State of New York for making her a bastard. Here's how it came about. The mother was a patient in a state mental hospital, where she was raped, conceived, and gave birth. The mother won her suit against the state for not keeping her safe from assault, but Baby W lost out when the court decided that life was better than no life at all. So much for the stigma.

The major questions, then, are: who will take care of the child, and how are his rights and yours affected by your having him single? How about the mother's right to receive the father's share of child support and the child's right to be supported? How about the child's right to inherit from both of his parents? Can the child receive the father's pension benefits, social security, life insurance? Does the father have the right to visit the child after you call it quits? Does the father have the right to custody when the parents separate or the mother dies? Here are just a few questions that you ought to consider right now. Now, before you go to bed. NOW, before the drugstore closes.

Since most consortiums do not contemplate the birth of children, we should understand the laws available for bastard prevention. The first means available is the developing law regarding abortion.

ABORTION

Until January 1973, when the Supreme Court at last decided the landmark abortion case, the state laws made procuring abortion, committing an abortion, aiding to commit abortion, and, of course, having an abortion a crime. Only highly limited exceptions existed. In most states, abortion was accepted in order to save the life of the mother. In others, the exception was expanded to allow lawful abortion on a physician's certification that the fetus was seriously defective. In still other states, an additional exception existed for pregnancies resulting from rape. The right-to-life versus the right-to-live debate is beyond the scope of this book. What follows is an outline of the condition of abortion law at this moment (with the warning that since the debate is still hot and heavy, the law may change between today, as this is written, and the day you read this in type).

When the United States Supreme Court confronted the abortion question brought to it by a pregnant single woman, the justices threaded their way through the history of anti-abortion law in the course of writing a scholarly decision they knew would hit the fan. Reaching back to ancient Greek and Roman theses and the writings of the top gynecologist of his time, "Doctor" Soranos, an Ephesian, they found that abortion was a recognized medical procedure. But, skipping ahead to about 400 B.C., they found that the Hippocratic Oath absolutely opposed abortion: "I will give no deadly medicine to anyone if asked, nor suggest any such counsel; and in like manner, I will not give to a woman a pessary to produce abortion." But it seems that Hippocrates was not in step with his times on this subject and that Plato and Aristotle commended abortion. English common law allowed legal abortion anytime before "quickening," which seems to have meant that abortion was accepted during the first trimester or until the first kick.

It was not until the Victorian era, in 1861, that abortion in the first trimester became a crime in England. The English law was later clarified to make abortion a crime only when the "child [was] capable of being born alive" and excused abortion if it was performed to preserve the life of the mother. And it was not until the 1950s that abortion statutes in the United States banned abortion at any stage in the pregnancy whether or not there was "quickening" and whether or not the first day or first trimester had passed. So the anti-abortion statutes held unconstitutional by the United States Supreme Court were more stringent than the ancient statutes and more "Victorian" than the Victorian statute.

In January 1973 the Supreme Court held that we, the people, have a constitutional right of privacy encompassing the right of a woman to decide whether or not to terminate her pregnancy. *But* the right is a qualified one. In the first trimester, the right is the woman's and the performing of the operation is between her and her doctor. In the stage after the first trimester, states can regulate toward the protection of the mother (but not the fetus. But subsequent to viability, the ability of the fetus to live independent of the mother, the state can make abortion a crime as in the old days.

Any hot Supreme Court decision produces the following results: (1) speeches by governors, speeches by congressmen, speeches in state legislatures, and speeches, speeches, speeches; (2) marches, demonstrations, letter-writing, self-appointed leaders, placards, newsletters, and fund-raising; and (3) more cases interpreting what the decision really said, more cases to get a reversal, more cases to find loopholes, and more cases, more cases, more cases. This decision was no exception.

The next Supreme Court decision held that physicians did not have to perform abortions. They could exercise their medical judgment to refuse abortion for just about any reason, the woman's age, the woman's health, including "physical, emotional, psychological, familial" so that the physician has the room to use his best judgment "for the benefit of the pregnant woman." But the Court did strike as unconstitutional a variety of "regulations" enacted to chill the decision to abort, including a state residency requirement, hospital staff approval, concurrence of two physicians, and so forth. Since those decisions, we have cases holding that purely private hospitals can refuse to allow abortions on the premises, that states cannot impose unreasonable or unduly restrictive licensing regulations on doctors performing abortions and on hospitals and clinics where abortions are performed, and that publicly operated hospitals cannot refuse to allow abortion. So the war goes on with state houses passing laws designed to sneak around the Supreme Court and the courts holding them unconstitutional. For example, Rhode Island passed a law declaring that life begins at conception, and thus they could regulate, that is prevent, abortion at any time. (Sorry, Rhode Island, that was unconstitutional. There is no fooling around with the first trimester.)

Then came a line of cases raising the question whether a woman may have an abortion without the consent of the unborn's father. The answer now pronounced by the Supreme

Court has been a resounding "yes." So far, the cases have held that neither the husband *nor* the father have any right to consent or withhold consent. This is a long step forward from ancient Greek and Roman times when abortion was never prosecuted as a crime except on the complaint of the father that his right to offspring was violated. And minors may have abortions without parental consent. A Delaware girl had the right to opt for abortion even though her parents refused consent, and she was all of twelve years old. So it can fairly be said that, at the present time, the woman engaging in consortium who finds herself pregnant can opt for abortion and she can exercise that option even without her consort's consent.

If neither abortion nor parenthood are acceptable in your consortium, the next procedure to consider is the completion of the pregnancy and birth and consent to adoption.

ADOPTION

Adoption can be a complicated legal procedure for the adoptive parents, including waiting lists, social workers' investigations, lawyers and the appointment of *guardian ad litem* (that is a lawyer hired by the court, but paid for by the adoptive parents, to represent the interests of the baby), the impounding of the original birth certificate, the issuance of a new birth certificate, and the issuance of a court decree declaring them lawful parents.

On the other hand, for the natural mother who is consenting to adoption, the legal procedure is quite simple. Usually the decision is made during pregnancy when the expectant mother tells her doctor that she plans to give up the child for adoption. The baby is born, and right at the hospital the social service agencies appear with the address of the appropriate office for the signing of consents. The consent is a short form wherein the mother acknowledges that she freely and willingly agrees to turn the child over to the appointed agency for adoption. That's it. Once the decision is made, and that may be difficult, the execution of the decision is easy. There are instances of adoption without the natural mother's consent, cases of extreme neglect or abandonment, but these are rare.

But what about the father? Is he left out of the decision-making process here as he was in abortion? Does he have the right to withhold his consent and prevent the adoption of his child? The answer is a resounding "maybe." And here, too, the law is changing right along with society's moods. It used to be that people were either married or single. Married people had babies and kept them. If a single woman got pregnant, it was a scandal and a mistake corrected by an illegal, backroom abortion — or she hid in her room or got out of town until the baby was born and adoption consents signed. It happened on occasion that a woman kept her bastard offspring. But the instance in which a father might take an interest in the child and really want to keep it was so rare that the law ignored this possibility. Now, though, with consortium, it is to be expected, or hoped, that single fathers will not conceal their identities and that they may even want to keep their own offspring. Thus, the law is going to have to deal with their rights, too.

In 1970, the Supreme Court of Wisconsin was presented with a petition by a father seeking his child from a state social service agency. The petitioner was a father of a two-year-old boy, a bastard. After the parents' consortium broke up, and for reasons of her own, the mother consented to the adoption of the child. He was living at the agency awaiting a possible placement when his father filed a petition seeking custody of his own child. In a hair-raising decision, the judges held that the mother only is the natural guardian of an illegitimate child and has rights superior to the father or anyone else because of her assumed "maternal care." Pointing out that the common law was carried forward in the statutes and that the word "parent" is defined to mean *mother* where bastards are involved, the court continued the old law that the mother alone has the power to terminate parental rights of a bastard and her consent to adoption is all that matters. The father has no standing to object, no right even to notification of the adoption. In deciding the case as it did, the Supreme Court of Wisconsin was acting in total consistency with the law as it had been for years, perhaps centuries.

While that case was being decided in Wisconsin, another man was fighting out his right to the custody of his illegitimate children in the Illinois courts. And therein lay the making of another radical change from the common law and another landmark decision where bastards are concerned. Joan and Peter lived together in consortium for eighteen years. In all respects their personal relationship was a marriage, although legally they were single. Since Illinois is not a state which recognizes common-law marriage, it did not matter that they lived together for as long as they did and that Joan was known by Peter's last name and that they had two children together that Peter acknowledged as his own, lived with, cared for, and loved. What did matter, as it turned out, is that no marriage license was ever issued to them and that no one ever said the magic words to legalize the union. Then Joan died. The state stepped in and made the children its wards, took custody of them, and arranged to place them for adoption. Peter fought his case to the Illinois Supreme Court, which applied the historical precedent and held that unwed fathers have no more right to their children than they would if they were total strangers. Peter then took his case to the United States Supreme Court, urging that he was the object of sex discrimination. And the United States Supreme Court agreed that Peter had been denied constitutionally guaranteed equal protection of the laws. The Court held that the interest of a man "in the children he has sired and raised, undeniably warrants deference and . . . protection." The Court also recognized that the state has the right to separate children from an unfit parent.

Was Peter joyfully united with his kids the day the Supreme Court read its decision? No. The state went back to court claiming he was unfit, partly because of his "immoral" living arrangements with Joan. The Illinois adoption act defines unfitness to include abandonment, extreme neglect, extreme and repeated physical cruelty, *and* open and notorious *fornication*. And the last news of this case was more years of court proceedings, more attorneys' fees, more court costs. This is not to say, though, that Peter's case was not important. It is indeed a landmark. That Supreme Court decision, rendered in 1972, recognizes at least that the male half of a consortium has some parental rights.

If the state claims he is unfit, it must prove it; it cannot ignore the father or treat him as if he were a stranger. And many states, because of Peter's landmark decision, have enacted laws which require that the father be notified if the mother consents to adoption, so that he may come into court and make his claim if he wants to keep his child. Still lurking behind the scenes, though, in every father's fight for his illegitimate child is the fear that the state will argue and prove that he is unfit and that the court will then place the child with another. In the future, it seems likely that fathers will keep their children as against the claims of the state if the *only* evidence of "unfitness" is that they didn't marry the mother. Further, it appears that they will lose their children if the evidence is that they didn't marry *and* that they abandoned the child, didn't support, acknowledge, or care for the child, or were otherwise of doubtful character (for example, convicted felons or drug users). It also seems likely that if the mother of a bastard dies, stating in her will that she wanted guardianship in someone other than the father, the court may give more weight to that direction than if the parents were legally married.

Consortium, then, is a risky business for fathers who want assurance that they will keep their kids when the mother consents to their adoption or dies. And if it's risky between the natural father and a stranger, does the father have a chance in a custody fight when the consortium breaks up? Because consortium is still new and the idea of the unmarried man staying with his bastard is considered revolutionary, there is not one reported case of a custody fight between breaking-up unmarried parents over their illegitimate child.

The only comparison is in divorce cases. There the law on child custody is that the best interests of the child govern which parent gets the child. For years mothers had the decided edge in custody battles, the judges assuming that "maternal instinct" and the societal pressures on little girls to play with their baby dolls and grow up to be good mamas meant that, in most cases, the maternal choice would be in the best interests of the child. But in divorce cases the law is changing to keep pace with women's liberation: the courts are slowly coming to place the contesting parents on an equal footing, without sexist preconceptions, to determine which parent will better assure the best interests of the child. These decisions pertain to a divorce where there has been a valid legal marriage, a legitimate child, and presumed "moral" parents. Is the analogy to consorts fighting custody a fair one? Will the judges revert to the common-law position that the mother is the only parent who counts where bastards are concerned and decide in favor of the mother? Or will the judges revert to the cliché of the double standard and presume that a woman who gives birth to a bastard is unfit to keep it, making the father the winner? The law doesn't yet have the answers. At the least, consorts who risk having children are treading untested waters.

Against this background, it is hardly surprising that there seems to be little hope for the consortium that wants to adopt a baby "in," as its own. Obviously, just about any married couple can have a baby. No one cares about your age, health, wealth, education, home environment. It takes extreme cruelty, violence, incest, starvation, battered child syndrome, abandonment, for the state to step in and try to remove a natural child from its parents. But adoption is different. Adoptive parents are screened, investigated, interviewed, and often anxious lest the child turned over to them pending the final decree for adoption may be snatched away. No baby ever looks as fat, healthy, happy, and well-dressed as the baby carried into court for a final adoption decree.

In the last ten years or so, a movement has been afoot to place single people on an equal legal footing with married people. As part of that movement, many states have revised their adoption laws to allow a single person to adopt a child. Single people living alone have, upon occasion, been successful in adopting older children and children from ethnic minority groups. But, single or married, the adoptive parent is subject to scrutiny for *unfitness*; with a single person adopting, it is more likely that the adoptive parent is subject to scrutiny for *imperfection*. This speculation is bolstered by the few cases where a single person attempted to adopt. You might succeed if you combine the attributes of Mary Poppins, Nelson Rockefeller, and Billy Graham. The odds are not good. And taking this to the next step, can a single couple adopt? The odds worsen geometrically. In the eyes of the law so far, you are not moral, conforming, stable, familial — and you are openly and notoriously fornicating and thus probably "unfit." You are not preventing but perpetuating the baby's status as bastard. His custody, support, and inheritance are in doubt. A consortium, for the present, is not going to succeed in adoption.

SUPPORT

Assuming, though, that you have a bastard, or that one is well on the way, or that you haven't been frightened off yet and you intend to have one, there is the question of responsibility for the child's support. Babies are cuddly, soft little bundles. They sleep (in cribs, then bunk beds, in apartments and houses); they eat (mother's milk, then strained vegetables, then hot dogs, then filet mignon); they wet their diapers, they tear the knees of their overalls, they dress in jeans and shoes and winter coats. They learn from Mommy and Daddy and Sesame Street and med school. And none of this is cheap. Married parents have a joint obligation to support their children. The divorced parent with custody can get a court order compelling child support, and the penalty for nonsupport may be imprisonment.

Under common law, the father had no privileges and no duties toward the bastard. There was no duty placed on the father of a bastard to support the child or give it his name. On the other hand, the mother, under common law, had all the privileges with regard to a bastard. She also had the duty of supporting it. The mother who failed to support her bastard child could be found guilty of criminal neglect. The father who didn't support his bastard child was merely a lucky bastard.

State legislatures, seeking to protect the illegitimate child (and trying to keep the welfare rolls down), have passed paternity laws. These laws provide that if a man is proven to be the father of a bastard he can be compelled to share with the mother in the support of the child. Their goal is to find a source of support for the bastard, preferably *not* as a ward of the state. Paternity cases establish support for the bastard and help for the mother in payment of her costs for the hospital, doctor, and even the burial of a bastard who dies. Since these laws are created by specific statute and are contrary to the common law, which lets the father completely off the hook, the statute should be followed to the letter. This is not the area for do-it-yourselfers. *And* it is most certainly not an area in which men defend themselves. A paternity case is not only a civil suit — that is, a fight between individuals — it also has criminal implications — that is, a fight between "the People of the State" and the reputed father, with a possible criminal penalty and sentence to jail.

In some states, for example, when a paternity suit is filed, an arrest warrant automatically issues and the sheriff, instead of simply serving a summons, arrests the accused "father" and brings him before the court. Since the purpose of the paternity suit is to provide the bastard with support, a name, and possible inheritance — in other words, all the same financial benefits available to a child born in lawful wedlock — the suit is not intended to punish the male for having intercourse with the plaintiff, or for getting her pregnant, or for walking away from his bastard. The criminal penalties, therefore, are not to punish him for what he did, but to punish him for what he might do: if he's proven to be the father and doesn't pay the ordered support, then he goes to jail.

Paternity suits are, by their nature, very different from other types of lawsuits. While the defendant (the person sued, the defender against the charges) is always the putative father, the role of plaintiff (the person complaining, the bringer of the suit) may be filled by a variety of persons. For example, the mother may sue. But also, the state may sue just as in usual criminal cases: *The People of the State* v. *John Smith*. And there are cases where the bastard's maternal grandparents have brought paternity suits.

In fact, just about anyone who claims he's unjustly burdened with a bastard's support can sue the reputed father. If either the mother or the bastard are on welfare, the agency administering aid can bring the suit. In New York City, where welfare problems are legend, the commissioner of social services joined with a mother in a paternity suit. Somewhere along the tortuous, time-consuming, and boring litigation road, the mother not only lost interest but absolutely refused to cooperate and insisted that the case be closed. The social service people insisted that they could go on without her and the court agreed that the mother didn't have to be a party, or appear, or even cooperate. If a case could be established without her, the welfare people had the right to continue the fight on behalf of the baby, who stands to gain support until his majority, the right to bear his father's name, the right to inherit from his father's estate, the right to his father's workmen's compensation, Veterans Administration, and social security benefits. Incidentally, of course, the welfare people might lasso someone to take care of the bastard so they can scratch one name off the public aid lists.

As in all civil suits, paternity suits may be tried before a jury and evidence is presented by each side. First the plaintiff offers evidence that the defendant is the father, then the defendant seeks to rebut that evidence. The plaintiff has the burden of proof. That is, the mother must convince the jury that the defendant is the father by the preponderance or greater weight in the evidence.

Let's see what kind of evidence each side can and cannot use. For the mother, the best possible evidence to bring before the jury and melt their hearts is the child himself. Thus confronted, juries are asked if this innocent is to be left without a name, without support, a bastard. How can a man, even an impotent, sterile man out of town at the time of conception, defend himself against a baby? Acknowledging the edge held by the baby, the law in many states is that the bastard is excluded from the courtroom, never to be seen by the jury. But the child may be strong evidence of paternity. While he can't testify as to who is his daddy, he can smile his crooked smile, peek out of his gray eyes, nod his curly red head, and wave his freckled hand across the courtroom at Daddy, who scowls his crooked scowl, lowers his gray eyes, turns away his curly red head, and hides behind his freckled fist. Resemblance may be meaningful evidence, but still, because of the prejudicial effect of having the child in the court, even that evidence has been excluded.

The next kind of evidence is the blood test. The doctor performs the blood test of the alleged father, mother, and baby. *But*, if the test proves the defendant could have been the father, most states will exclude it. The only blood test evidence that can be used is if the test proves conclusively that the man could *not* have been the father.

Recently, a North Carolina jury heard a paternity case in which the only evidence on the plaintiff's side was the mother's testimony. In a quiet, frightened voice she testified that Samuel and only Samuel could be the father as it was only he that she had ever slept with. A tear dripped down her cheek; the jury sighed. Samuel also had only one witness, Dr. R., who testified that he had performed blood tests and found that the mother was Type O, the defendant was Type O, and the baby was Type

A, and that it is absolutely impossible for O plus O to produce an A. Samuel could not have been the father, he stated scientifically and unequivocally, but the jury was thinking of the sweet young mother, the bastard, and the welfare their taxes would pay. Science, M.D.'s, and Mendel's laws went down the drain. The jury found Samuel guilty and he was sentenced to jail unless he paid support. An appeal followed and the North Carolina judges held that Mendel was more reliable than the jury. Sam went free.

How then does the mother or the state or the welfare office prove its case when resemblance hardly counts and blood tests can help only the defendant? The plaintiff relies on all the evidence available. That the man took the child as a dependent on his tax return has some weight; that the man paid the obstetrician, hung around the hospital, supported the baby for a while carries more weight; that the man handed out cigars and admitted paternity to third persons is also good evidence. The man may, under oath on the witness stand, admit to the affair at the crucial time. Some states allow the man to take the Fifth Amendment so that he need not testify and no inferences can be drawn from his refusal to testify. Other states say that the Fifth Amendnent cannot protect him and he must testify. And last, but certainly not least, there is the evidence of the reputation of the mother for promiscuity. How many men has she slept with? How many men in the month of conception?

A court in the Bronx refused to find paternity in the defendant when the plaintiff, the mother, reluctantly admitted to having four other bastards with four other men, and her testimony indicated that she had five or six male friends at the crucial time. Therein lies the old college fraternity game: defend a paternity case by bringing in the entire fraternity chapter to testify that each member slept with the plaintiff. In the first place, it's not a nice game; in the second place, it's perjury; in the third place, it has no relevance to single people living together in a true consortium.

In a few states, paternity suits may provide no relief at all to parties in consortium. Those paternity statutes predate the present notions of consortium and the statutes assumed that no relationship existed between plaintiff-mother and defendant-father except a quick act of sex and the man running out on the announcement that his girl is "in trouble." Let's assume that two people live together, have a bastard, and stay together. Years pass and then the consortium goes on the rocks. He leaves without any intention to provide support to his bastard. She brings a paternity suit to force him to share in the obligations. In those few states, the paternity laws have statutes of limitations which say, for example, that unless a paternity suit is brought within two years of the bastard's birth, the suit is barred forever. So, in a consortium which continues, paternity suits may not help. You'd better get together on a genuine, written acknowledgment of paternity, and it must be said that the very best protection for the bastard is still old-fashioned ordinary divorceable marriage.

INHERITANCE

At common law, a bastard could inherit only from his mother. Even taking into account the revolutionary changes of today, basically that is *still* the law.

In order to understand the impact (or lack of impact) of this, we'll digress a minute from bastards and talk a bit about death. Cautious, careful, conservative types work and save for themselves and their posterity. Even of that group, probably only a small percentage think of paying a lawyer to draft a will. Those who have a legally valid will can leave their estates to practically anyone and they can disinherit practically anyone too.* The only ones who must inherit something are surviving spouses, who in most states are guaranteed a certain percentage (usually one-third) of their spouse's estate, and of course the govern-

---

* For details on the passing of property by will, and inheritance and disinheritance of bastards named in wills, see Chapter 9.

ment, which always "inherits" its share of death taxes. But children, even legitimate children, in all but a very few states, can be completely disinherited. "To my son, Joey, who quit school to join a commune, I give one dollar" — and that's it, Joey, live it up. "To my daughter, Shirley, who is living with a man she isn't married to and who said I would never remember her in my will, hello Shirley." On the other hand, people who have valid wills can endow anyone: "To the bank teller, Mary Smith, who always smiled at me when I made a deposit, I give one million dollars." The newspapers love to write up these items, which are inspirations to thousands of bank tellers everywhere.

So when we talk about a bastard's right to inheritance, we are not talking about their right to receive property under wills. If named a beneficiary in a will (except in a few states), the bastard collects along with everyone else. We are talking, rather, about the laws of "intestate succession." While valid wills cover the passing of property on the death of the will-writer, the "testate," the laws of intestate succession govern the passage of property for the rest of us clods who don't have wills. Every state has these laws and they set forth the table of heirship — that is, the way property passes on death. For example, if the deceased has a wife and children, one-third of his property goes to his wife and two-thirds to his children. If no wife, then it all goes to the kids; if no kids and no wife and no grandchildren, then to the parents of the deceased; if no parents then to his sisters and brothers, if no sisters and brothers then to nieces and nephews, if no nieces and nephews then to aunts and uncles, and so on. Every state has its own formula. And every state has special rules for bastards.

In many states the law of intestate succession provides that "an illegitimate child" inherits only from his mother or his maternal grandparents, or anyone else through whom his mother might inherit, but an illegitimate child does not inherit from his father or his father's side of the family *unless* the child has been legitimatized by the marriage of his mother and father. Some states let bastards inherit from the father who acknowledges himself to be the father, in writing, in the presence of witnesses, even though he doesn't marry the bastard's mother; but then, while the bastard can inherit from his father, he can't inherit from his other paternal relatives. Some states let bastards inherit from their fathers and their father's side of the family, without marriage of the parents but with written acknowledgement of paternity signed in the presence of a justice of the peace. Still other states authorize the bastard to inherit, as if legitimate, from the father and the father's family *if* the father and mother marry *and* the father acknowledges the bastard as his own.

Se each state contributes to the confusion, all in the name of the state's right to encourage marriage and discourage people from having bastards. These variations come together in the courts where they have to be unscrambled. For example, L.C.S. was killed in a steam explosion in the Manhattan office building where he worked. The parents of L.C.S. brought a wrongful-death personal-injury suit in New York against the building owners and others, and stood to recover a large amount of money which they claimed for themselves. L.C.S. had no will and the proceeds of the suit would therefore pass by the laws of intestate succession. L.C.S. was unmarried, but as it turned out, L.C.S. had a bastard daughter whom he had acknowledged in a signed statement appended to her birth certificate. The baby was born in Florida and lived there; because her domicile was Florida, questions as to her personal status were governed by Florida law. The decedent was killed in New York, but lo and behold, he was a commuter: he lived in New Jersey, and that was his domicile and he was governed by New Jersey law. The passage of the New York suit proceeds were governed by the law of the decedent's domicile, New Jersey, which recognized that an illegitimate would be treated as legitimate if the steps taken at the child's domicile had that effect. The Florida law held that the written acknowledgment gave the child the right to inherit; that was honored in New Jersey; New York acknowledged New Jersey, and the proceeds of the wrongful death suit went to the bastard and not her grandparents.

When the United States Supreme Court got a case in 1968, a little sun started to shine on the bastards of this country. Ms. L. died and her administrator claimed that her death was caused by the negligence of the hospital and the doctors who treated, or mistreated, her in her last illness. Ms. L. had five illegitimate children on whose behalf the suit was brought. The state court held that while the bastards could inherit from their mother whatever she owned when she died, they could not sue to recover for wrongful death. The state court tossed out their claim on the basis of a statute which denied bastards the right to recover, "based on morals and general welfare because it discourages bringing children into the world out of wedlock." Yes, that's what the state court said.

The Supreme Court decided that there was something wrong with (1) letting wrongdoers go free because the plaintiffs were bastards, and (2) denying legal rights to children because they were born illegitimate, and that the bastards were just as injured by their mother's death as legitimate kids would have been. Therefore, the kids were being denied the equal protection of the laws and the state had acted unconstitutionally.

Then the Supreme Court took the next step forward. A young man, a bastard, was killed in an automobile accident and the bastard's mother brought a suit to recover damages for her son's wrongful death. Again the state court denied her the right to sue because to do so would encourage "sin." But the Supreme Court didn't see that it would prevent sin to allow the mother to recover for the death of her illegitimate son. Would more women give birth to bastards because they could be compensated in damages for their wrongful death? The equal protection clause of the Constitution protects against such arbitrary classifications.

Bastards are not out of the woods yet, however. The Supreme Court in 1971 had its chance to make bastards equal to legitimate children, but refused. Ezra died intestate, without a will, leaving an assorted bunch of cousins, uncles, and other "collateral" relatives. "Collateral" relatives are those several steps removed from "lineal" relatives — parents, spouses, children — in the laws of intestate succession. Ezra also was survived by a daughter. If she were legitimate, Ezra's daughter would have received his entire estate. But because she was a bastard she received nothing, and the collaterals shared the entire estate. In support of this holding, the Supreme Court said that Ezra's state law provided several ways in which Ezra could have legitimatized his daughter, but he did none of them. It also said that the state may have chosen a pattern of intestate succession which had some faults, but that was up to the state. There was nothing unconstitutional in what the state had done. Since this case, state courts have found new support for their denials of paternal inheritance to bastards even where the father had acknowledged the child or had been proven to be the father in a paternity suit. These courts say, of course, that if the father wanted his illegitimate child to inherit along with his legitimate child all he had to do was write a will — *or* marry the bastard's mother.

So it is that the bastard is on the outside, not a genuine child, not a full-fledged sibling, and with very little help available to him. There is no busing of bastards to integrate them. There are not bastard antidefamation leagues. All of which means that you will have to think a bit harder and plan a bit longer if your consortium decides to be fruitful and multiply.

3. Criminal Law Violations

Isn't it enough that your mother hasn't spoken to you since you told her you had entered into a consortium? Isn't it enough that your married friends consider your relationship to be a fling and offer to fix you up — object: matrimony? Among all of the other stumbling blocks to consortium lurks the possibility of criminal prosecution.

Consortium is a crime in just about every state of the Union. But take heart. Consortium is a crime because fornication, adultery, and sodomy are crimes. The "criminal element" is everywhere: our neighbors, our friends, our cousins, our doctors, lawyers, judges, and even our politicians who declaim against the rampant crime wave. Of all of the problems discussed in this book, the violation of the criminal laws is the only one that can land you in jail. But so rare is the enforcement of these laws that you can surely sleep well, and together, tonight after reading about them.

Because there are so many labels for sexual conduct, the legal definitions compel a brief examination:

Fornication is sexual intercourse between persons not married to each other.

Adultery is sexual intercourse between persons, one or both of whom are married to others.

Cohabitation is living together single.

Fellatio is oral stimulation of the male sex organ.

Cunnilingus is oral stimulation of the female sex organ.

Sodomy originally meant anal intercourse between men but now is variously defined to include anal intercourse with a woman, fellatio, cunnilingus, and bestiality (copulation between a human being and an animal).

Also included in the criminal statutes are homosexuality, necrophilia (a sexual attraction to corpses), and buggery (which sometimes means bestiality and sometimes means fellatio and cunnilingus). The ambiguity of these terms stems from the shyness of the early legislators who used them but refused to tell us what they meant. In fact when John H. was convicted of a "crime against nature," the supreme court freed him because the language was so vague the court wasn't sure what it meant.

Although we tend to take the "criminality" of these acts lightly, this is not reflected in the punishments which may be doled out. These are not only severe, but also inconsistent between the states and illogical as related to the "illegal act." For example, male homosexual conduct may result in imprisonment, but lesbianism is often not even a crime. Anal intercourse carries a maximum sentence of twenty years, oral intercourse, three years. A single act of sexual intercourse between unmarried people (fornication) is punishable by imprisonment in more than a dozen states and by fines in others. Adultery historically (and biblically) was a crime of married *women* only. A married man could fool around with impunity. Now adultery is defined in the United States as relating to either married partner, but some foreign countries still retain the distinction. Severe and regularly enforced punishments exist in every state when a partner to the sexual act is a child. This is serious business. Be sure your consort is of age.

While criminal prosecution of most of these types is rare, cases are still brought. Generally the prosecutions are initiated by a hurt and vengeful spouse (in Iowa, the only way adultery can be prosecuted is on the complaint of the "innocent" spouse) or by a prosecutor with an ax to grind. In a recent case, a man was charged with fornication after the prosecution found itself in the awkward position of losing after a celebrated trial. Mr. S. was arrested and charged with rape and assault with intent to rape after he and a friend had picked up two women at a supermarket parking lot. The evidence proved that the women had gone with the men on a purely voluntary basis, fooled around in their car, and engaged in a variety of sexual acts all absolutely willingly. Some hours after the "victims" left the car, and after they felt remorse over their evening out, they filed a complaint charging Mr. S. and his friend with assault and rape. The men were arrested and each man spent seven months in jail awaiting trial. During the trial, Mr. S. testified fully to having fornicated with the "victim." As the trial progressed toward conclusion, it became more and more clear that the jury would acquit, so the judge on his own initiative charged Mr. S. with fornication. The jury acquitted on the rape charges, but of course found Mr. S. guilty of fornication. He had freely admitted as much. Mr. S. argued that criminal fornication statutes were unconstitutional because of their unequal application and the invasion of the right of privacy inherent in them. Evidence was offered through psychologists, sociologists, sex surveyors, and statisticians, who told the judge what they learned and everyone else knows anyway. Sex is more popular than ever. Society is more permissive. Adultery is admitted daily in divorce court and almost never criminally prosecuted. "Sexual tensions," they said, "resulting from the proscription of sexual activity, whether moral or legal, result in personality problems traceable to those proscriptions . . . [and] guilt feelings and anxiety are created . . ." A study elicited the fact that even prosecutors favor repeal of these criminal statutes, although the State Division of Criminal Justice's reponse to the survey was "this office has no experience in fornication." Finally, the widely held view was that "fornication and cohabitation are crimes punishable by marriage." It doesn't matter, said the judge. The state has the right to regulate sexuality, to prevent the birth of bastards, to impede the contagion of venereal disease. Mr. S. was fined $50 and his conviction for the high crime of fornication stands.

The ever-vigilant sheriff's office of the Commonwealth of Virginia sought to spare us a shock to our consciences by arresting Elsie and Clarence and charging them with "gross lewdness and lasciviousness," for which they were fined $300 each. It seems that the citizens had complained about the carrying-on at the Glen Plaid, a motel converted to efficiency apartments. Three deputy sheriffs conducted a surveillance of the premises for two months. Finally, through a sheer curtain of a back room they spied Elsie standing nude. They watched her for some time and then seeing Clarence asleep in bed, made their move and arrested them both. And so justice was done and we can all rest easier tonight.

Notwithstanding these examples, charges of sexual "crimes" between two consenting adults in private are seldom made (particularly when one realizes how widespread is the "crime"). Moreover, many courts will go to extremes to find the accused "innocent." Many potential cases are never brought because the prosecutor is not interested in adding these "victories" to his record. Others are dismissed by judges' strict construction of the statutes involved. In other cases, the jury will not convict for a "crime" that does the public no harm and of which they themselves may be guilty.

In still other instances, the court is moved by the basic unfairness of hand-picking one out of potential thousands for prosecution. When Jane C. applied for public aid for her three illegitimate children, she was compelled by the Welfare Department to identify their father, Charles B., and to bring a paternity suit against him. The state insisted on that identification of the father and the bringing of a paternity suit in order to impose support obligations on the father, thus lightening the welfare load. After she identified Charles and he was proven to be the father in the paternity suit, the state filed criminal charges against them both. Jane was sentenced to a six-month jail term, suspended. Charles was sentenced to spend three months in jail. They filed their appeals and both sentences were reversed. The judge held that there was a basic unfairness in conditioning the receipt of welfare funds for needy children on their mother's identifying the father and cooperating in a suit against him, and then, having incriminated herself, seeing the state turn around and charge her with a crime. The court held that the state could not force mothers to identify the father and bring paternity suits against them as a condition to the receipt of welfare funds for their children. If, however, the mother did so cooperate with the state, she was to be immune from criminal prosecution for the sexual acts that brought her to need public aid in the first place.

Until 1967, the New York criminal code made "consensual sodomy" an offense. So it was a crime for two consenting adults in private, whether they were single or a married couple in the privacy of their own bedroom, to engage in "deviate sexual intercourse," which the statute defined as "consisting of contact between the penis and anus, the mouth and penis, or the mouth and vulva." In a step toward awareness, liberality, modernity, and radical chic, the statute was amended. After the amendment, the "crime" remained a crime, but only when engaged in by persons *not* married to each other.

Ms. J., an unmarried woman, was indicted for the crime of consensual sodomy. The judge of the upstate New York court dismissed the charges, holding that they were unconstitutionally discriminatory against single people. The judge pointed out that the particular statute is not concerned with "compulsion, duress, public view, or prostitution," but only makes "criminals of some citizens, but not others" because the former are single and the latter are married. On the other hand, the court did agree that the statute would be proper and enforceable if it was directed at the same conduct, but by persons of the same sex. So, while most sexual conduct between consenting adults in private is no longer tainted with criminality, homosexuals are still subject to a separate standard.

The criminal laws regarding homosexuality are as confused and inconsistent as society is in dealing with homosexuals. In some jurisdictions anal intercourse is a far more serious offense than cunnilingus, and therefore male homosexuals are subject to long prison terms while lesbians are not. The trend is definitely toward the removal of criminal sanction from all sexual conduct between consenting adults in private, whether they be heterosexual or homosexual. But as recently as March 1976, the Supreme Court ruled that states may prosecute and imprison people for committing homosexual acts, even when both parties to an act are consenting adults and the act occurs in private. Although prosecutions are infrequent, even consortium for homosexuals, under existing law, is a risk. Grave distinctions between heterosexual and homosexual do continue to exist. For example, it is perfectly acceptable for a heterosexual couple to meet in a bar, exchange the usual chit-chat, and work their way to bed. The homosexual must tread very carefully in a similar situation or he may be arrested for soliciting for homosexual activity.

And there is the potential of criminal indictment every time consorts take a vacation together. Nancy, who has an innocent face and hardly appears to be engaged in a life of crime, recounted the romantic beginning and sad ending to her consortium with Ted. Among the sensitive issues in their relationship was their travel arrangements. Ted did a lot of traveling in his business — that other people paid for. In each city, a hotel room was reserved for him in his name.

"Ted dropped me off near the hotel and I was supposed to — I did — walk around this strange downtown and look in store windows and walk up and down the aisles of the gift shop until enough time passed and I assumed he had checked in and was safely in his room. Then I'd phone him from the cigar stand, ask his room number, and go up. That's how we worked it. I never told him how infuriating this was. Sometimes, to get back at him, I'd kill time, stop for coffee, browse longer, before I called and came up."

Scott was matter-of-fact. Sure, he and Laura were living together, sure everyone knew about it. "If my boss doesn't like it, so what? I like it." But even Scott, when he and Laura went to Scottsdale, to that elegant resort hotel, checked in as "Mr. and Mrs." Traveling together is fraught with peril.

If you check into a hotel as Mr. and Mrs., or under assumed

names, you are committing a crime. Most states impose criminal penalties for false registration at hotels. On the other hand, if you register in your own names, the hotel may not accept you. And that is not just because the hotel management is narrow-minded. It is because the management is subject to criminal penalty if it registers a single man and woman in the same room. The crime is "keeper of a disorderly house" and may mean license revocation, fine, or imprisonment. Then, to top it all, you can't legally register just one name and have your consort sneak in later, as Nancy did. You are also cheating the hotel out of its double-occupancy rate, adding dishonesty to the offense. The alternative is that each of you registers separately in a separate room, you pay the exorbitant two-room rate, and one sneaks into the other's room, subjecting you to criminal prosecution for fornication and to the hotel's rancor at being itself exposed to prosecution (the rancor is greatly quieted by the receipt of the extra rate, though).

When planning to travel together in Europe, remember that the hotelkeepers check and hold your passports. Whether you will succeed in staying in the same room depends on the country and the particular hotel. Best to check ahead.

There is no question but that traveling together in consortium is more difficult and more expensive than traveling together in marriage. At this writing, the airlines and the Civil Aeronautics Board have abandoned the husband-and-wife "family plan" rates, but when they were in effect, a wife traveled at lower price with her husband. Thus the harried housefrau of the television commercial could implore, "Take me along," knowing that her prayer was bolstered by an airline's reduced fare. But that bonus was not available to a consort who forthrightly sought to be taken along under her own name.

As if all this weren't complicated enough, there lurks the Mann Act too. That act, passed by Congress in 1910 and officially known as "The White Slave Traffic Act," makes it a crime, punishable by fine and imprisonment, to knowingly transport a woman in "interstate commerce" (across a state line) for the purpose of prostitution *or* debauchery *or* "any other immoral practice," even if she wants to go. The United States Supreme Court found the act constitutional and upheld convictions even though the man employed no force, there was no commercial scheme (prostitution), there was nothing more than a man traveling with a woman for the "immoral purpose" of her being his "concubine or mistress." The Supreme Court approved the position that "The prostitute may, in the popular sense, be more degraded in character than the concubine, but the latter nonetheless must be held to lead an immoral life." Granted, this is the Supreme Court of 1917 and not today. But in 1960 the Supreme Court was given another chance to void the act, or limit it to instances of prostitution, and it did not.

Lower courts in more recent years have been far more permissive in their interpretation of the Mann Act. In 1960, when Mr. M. was charged with crossing from West Virginia to Louisiana with a woman, for the purpose of "engaging in sexual intercourse and other sexual acts with her," the court dismissed the indictment, pointing out that the woman was a consenting adult and that fornication is not illegal in Louisiana; therefore they were not going to commit an illegal act but only an "immoral act," which is indefinable. Still the Mann Act is on the books. Congress has neither repealed it nor rewritten it. The Supreme Court has still held it enforceable. It is not to be ignored.

Whether, however, the statutes against fornication, sodomy, fellatio, cunnilingus, transportation across state lines, false registration into hotels, and so forth are actually going to ruin your plans for a skiing trip to Aspen is up to you. The actual risk of criminal prosecution is small, but the laws are there.

4. Consortium and Divorce

WAS JACK telling the truth when he said (in the presence of his consort) that he was more faithful to his consort — or at least more careful — than he had been with his wife?

"If my wife was angry because I didn't come home, well, she was mad, but she didn't run to a lawyer. Divorce is such a hassle. But if I don't show up here, Naomi could just walk out. I wouldn't risk it."

Naomi purred.

Could Raymond be lying when he explained why he didn't unpack the moving cartons long after he had moved in with Sandi, even after his divorce was final?

"I know it's a mess, but it's permanent this time, and when I get around to unpacking I want everything put away where it's going to stay."

Sandi purred.

One thing was certainly true. Both Jack and Ray had been through a divorce — the legal proceeding, the only way (other than death) to end a marriage. I knew also that the consortium each had entered could end whenever they wanted it to end. No lawyers, no decrees, no alimony payments. They knew it too.

Ray had moved into Sandi's apartment the day he moved out of his house in the suburbs, but long before the decree for divorce was signed by the judge. *Long* before. Ray wanted his divorce; his wife didn't. It took her several months and a few visits, alone, to a marriage counselor to realize she couldn't keep him, not if he really wanted to go. In states with no-fault divorce statutes, Ray would have had only to go to court, state that there were irreconcilable differences and an irremediable breakdown of the marriage, and he could be divorced. The obligations as to alimony, child support, division of property would follow swiftly.

But Ray lives in a state which still has grounds for divorce. This meant that he had to prove that his wife was guilty of the kind of conduct that constituted grounds. He had to prove she was physically cruel, adulterous, a drunk, or, at the least, guilty of mental cruelty (serious misconduct directed at his physical or emotional well-being). He didn't love her but he couldn't prove the grounds. And even if he could, he wouldn't be divorced because he himself was guilty of adultery. His wife knew about Sandi; her lawyer knew about Sandi. If Ray had sued his wife for divorce, she could raise the defense called recrimination. That defense says that, if the seeker of the divorce is himself guilty of grounds for divorce, he cannot succeed. The marriage might have gone on forever. It ended only when Ray's wife realized that she couldn't have him back, and, much later, that she didn't want him back. Then the question resolved itself to a matter of money. Only when his wife was satisfied with the property arrangement did she agree to ask the court for a divorce.

Even Ray agrees that it wasn't a bad settlement. She waived alimony after all, got back into the job market, and works part-time. The child support is tough, but the kids are almost grown. She did get the house. The whole thing just took so many months, for which, of course, they blame the lawyer. "He sure took advantage of our situation. He's a very bitter man."

The wife's lawyer, Mr. R., was doing his job. Ray's wife had believed that she had Ray, her house, her stove, his credit status forever; after all, that's what she was reared to believe. She needed time to adjust, and Mr. R. provided it.

When they were divorced, Ray's wife calmly charged him with mental cruelty: "He was cold, sullen, morose, indifferent." She could have charged him with adultery and named Sandi as co-respondent. She didn't. She could have sued Sandi for alienation of affections. She didn't. Only two things would have been accomplished by such charges. Had she named Sandi as co-respondent, she would taste sweet revenge, with Sandi's name dragged through the proceedings as "the other woman, the homewrecker." Had she filed suit for alienation of affections, she might get a small, very small — and highly un- likely — award of money from Sandi. Mr. R., "that bitter man," had convinced her that it wasn't worth the trouble, that Ray would only rise to Sandi's defense, making future relations (timely child support payments, friendly visitation with the kids) difficult if not impossible. As time passed, she realized that all she wanted was a decent settlement and a peaceful di- vorce.

That is what usually happens. But the possibilities of being sued for alienation and being charged civilly (and criminally) with adultery are ever present for the consort of a married per- son. And the married half of the consortium may pay dearly for his pre-divorce living-together arrangement.

The problems created by consortium do not end with the di- vorce decree. Jean had custody of her eight-year-old daughter. The court had awarded custody to her, and rightly. She is a wise and loving parent. Her former husband is cold and more devoted to his work than to his child. But he is a proud man, a strait-laced one, too. When he learned that Jean was living with a man to whom she was not married, he moved for a change of custody. And he practically got it. Jean had to promise that she would be either married or living alone before the court would allow her to continue in her custody. There is a very real prob- lem in consortium. Married couples can do almost anything with regard to the care (or lack of it) of their children. The law is concerned only in the most serious battered-child or neglect cases. But custody following a divorce case is subject to the constant scrutiny of the judge, who determines what is in the best interests of the child. And judges, like almost everyone else in their age, education, and social status group, do not like consortium.

Those alimony payments which are going into the consortium rent, food, and utilities fund may also be taken away. There are two kinds of alimony. The first is lump sum alimony, which is a specified amount payable at one time or in installments until the sum is fully paid. Lump sum alimony is paid whether or not the person receiving it is married or consorting. It goes on until the sum is paid off and that's it. No more, no less. The second form of alimony is periodic alimony. These payments are at a fixed weekly or monthly amount but they go on until the recipient dies or remarries. The payments can therefore last months or decades. It is the receipt of the periodic alimony payment that is endangered in consortium.

The trend toward cutting off alimony to the person who is living in consortium is upward. And the trend is coinciding with a general move away from periodic alimony. Women are expected to be able to support themselves and they had better be able to do so. No case discussed in this section was decided earlier than 1974. Consortium is recent and the termination of alimony because of it is even more recent.

When Mr. and Mrs. G. were divorced, she got child custody and child support, alimony, and the right to live in the home until the youngest child completed high school. Then the house was to be sold, and the proceeds split. Before the child completed grammar school, Mrs. G. entered into a consortium. Her consort moved into the marital home and shared expenses. He provided money from his salary, Mrs. G. provided money from Mr. G., her alimony. When Mr. G. objected, the judge agreed and said that "To compel the ex-husband to contribute to his ex-wife's support would be, under the circumstance, to use the authority and power of this court to encourage crime and subsidize immorality." He ordered the termination of the alimony and the immediate sale of the home. (The judge did not transfer the child custody to Mr. G. Mr. G. never asked for it.)

The Illinois court faced with the same situation refused to terminate alimony but did agree to reduce it, because the former wife's financial needs were, at least in part, being provided by her consort. The Kentucky Court of Appeals has decided that the former wife's living with another does not release her husband from his alimony obligation. And the Florida court has also refused to terminate alimony to a woman living with a man in consortium, pointing out that "a ceremonial marriage offers various benefits, as well as legal rights, duties, and obligations, which do not obtain in the wife's relationship with Mr. S. He is under no obligation to support her or even stay with her, and she is neither entitled to dower or government social security benefits upon his death, nor is she recognized by the world at large as S's wife."

The battle rages on. Many courts are deciding this question. Many courts are disagreeing with each other. State legislatures are considering bills that provide that alimony will be vacated or reduced when the recipient "is living with a person of the opposite sex while unmarried." In growing numbers, divorce decrees ordering periodic alimony state that payments are "to continue until death or remarriage. The word 'remarriage' shall be deemed to include the wife's living with a man although not ceremonially or legally married to him."

So, along with the factors of love, loneliness, kindness, compassion, and sex that you consider in deciding whether consortium is for you, you may also have to consider charges of adultery, alienation of affections, loss of child custody and child support, the sale of your home, the termination of alimony — gone and never to be awarded again.

5. The Use of a Name

CAN THIS CHAPTER be written, short as it is, without quoting Shakespeare?

While the common-law principles on the use of a name are well-established in our legal history, and although every state has, and has had for many years, statutory procedures for official court-approved name changes, there is a new interest in this area of law. Part of the new concern comes out of the women's liberation movement. Married women are now deciding to revert to their maiden names, single women are electing to retain their maiden names when they marry, and married couples, affirming their individual identities (and perhaps moved by the classy sound), have taken to joining their individual names by hyphenating them. Another reason for concern about name change involves the adoption of religions or quasi-political, quasi-religious movements, with name changes being undertaken to identify membership — Cassius Clay to Muhammad Ali, Patricia to Tania. Still another cause for concern with names comes with the new family relationship. That is, a couple marries and they have children; the couple divorces, each remarries, they have children with their new spouses, who already have children from prior marriages and so forth, until the doorbell has a variety of names and it seems like a good idea, somewhere along the line, to unify the family with a uniform surname. Finally, a consort may want to adopt the other's name, or they may want to hyphenate their names, or they may want to settle on a name for their illegitimate children.

Under the common law, an adult may adopt any name he

chooses so long as he does so with no fraudulent intent. This means that a person may choose to call himself anything he wants to and that's it, that's his name. He can call himself Mickey Mouse, Clark Kent, or Superman, and once he makes that decision, he is Mickey Mouse, Clark Kent, or Superman. The only restriction on his lawful adoption of a name is that the name must not be chosen to defraud others. You can't choose the name of Rockefeller to use superb and undeserved credit and pass bum checks. You can't call yourself DeBeers to sell nonexistent diamond mines. You can't palm yourself off as Henry Kissinger to get a free ride on El Al.

Most important, what this also means is that if one of you adopts the other's name, you may be causing creditors to rely on the credit of your consort. Before you decide on a name change, you should decide whether you are willing to accept responsibility for your consort's debts. The "family expense statutes" and the common law make married spouses liable for the family-type debts of each other.* If one of you consents to allow the other to use your name, the consort is using your credit too, and a creditor may claim that you are responsible for expenses charged by your "spouse."

The statutory name-change procedure is not needed to carry out your intention to adopt your consort's name or to hyphenate your names or to return to your maiden name after a divorce. The statutory procedure is worthwhile though to straighten out the record with all of the official departments that have your name and serial number on their computers. It helps to go to court and have the judge decree your name change, so that your driver's license issues, your credit cards transfer to you with your own prior credit rating, social security knows who you are, the post office can deliver you mail, and people who owe you money can find you.

In most states the legal procedures for change of name are simple. First, the applicant for the change prepares a written

---

* For more on the family expense statutes and creditors' rights, see Chapter 6.

petition asking the judge to change his name. Then he publishes a notice in the legal notice section of the want ads once a week for several weeks (whatever the statute requires). The applicant then appears in court, and if no one responds to the notice with a valid objection to the change, the judge signs the decree and from that day on you have a new official label. As simple as that is, it is even easier for a woman to change her name in a divorce proceeding. There the divorce court judge can decree a return to maiden name at the same time as he grants her divorce decree.

Name changes are routinely granted in the courts every day. But occasionally a judge gets stubborn about approving a name change. On occasion, a judge will refuse to allow a newly liberated married woman to return to her maiden name. In one case, the judge refused to allow "an American-born citizen, disavowing the faith and tenets of his church," to accept a name prescribed by his adopted Eastern religion, although he acknowledged that the applicant, Mr. Green, had every right to accept any religion he chose. In a decision that reads like the lyrics to a George M. Cohan song, the judge refused to let Green deny his name, stating that he "should measure himself by the American standard and be proud not only of being an American citizen but manifest esteem for the honorable name by which he has been known for nigh a generation." The judge then went on to point out that the name Green "echoes in American politics, government, finance, in peace and in war. The Revolutionary War produced the Green Mountain boys, who so valiantly fought and died for their, and now our, glorious country. Their cause was a common bond in the formation of the greatest democracy known in the modern world. The blood spilled by the great American patriots should not be despoiled by strange and foreign adaptions. This birthright should not conceal itself behind such an alien shield. It has sufficient buoyancy to float upon the sea of time and in years to come the petitioner may hopefully add luster to the name of Green." Name change application denied. These judges who deny non-fraudulent name changes, are, perhaps, overly harsh. It seems a small exercise in free speech and the pursuit of happiness to choose a surname.

The subject of name changes is more complex where children are concerned. As the law now stands, the natural father of a legitimate, born-in-wedlock child has a right to have his child bear his name. Divorced women who have sought to change their children's surname to their own, or to the name of their present husband, have not been successful when the child's father objects.

Bastards, whose common-law history dictates that their rights (and the obligations to them) flow from their mothers, have their mother's surname.* The only ways a bastard's surname can be changed is by his mother's marriage to a man who consents to the child's having his name, or by adoption, or through the procedure of a paternity suit. Fathers of bastards are at last being allowed some rights, and some obligations as well. Nancy Jane had been married and divorced and then lived in a communal arrangement with three or four other young men and women before she settled into consortium with James J. After several months of consortium, Nancy Jane became pregnant. James urged Nancy Jane to obtain an abortion, but when she refused he "agreed to permit" Nancy Jane to name the child James J., Jr., "on the condition that she never seek to obtain support payments from him." Nancy Jane had the child, named him James J., Jr., and within a few months the consortium ended. James kept his end of the bargain. He neither cared for the child nor supported him. About five years later, Nancy Jane began living with Mr. C., whom she planned to marry "when and if his wife ever consents to a divorce." She and Mr. C. decided to change little James J., Jr.'s name to James C. and started the statutory legal proceedings to effect the change. When the natural father heard of the name change, he filed his objections. He wanted Junior to stay Junior. Lo and behold, he

---

* For more on bastards, see Chapter 2.

won, but he lost too. The child kept his father's name, but it seems that Daddy ended up paying some support too.

Although we may ask, "What's in a name? That which we call a rose by any other name would smell as sweet," perhaps Iago's observation is more to the point: "Good name in man and woman, dear my lord, is the immediate jewel of their souls; Who steals my purse steals trash; 'tis something, nothing; 'Twas mine, 'tis his, and has been slave to thousands; But he that filches from me my good name robs me of that which not enriches him, and makes me poor indeed." Or, with all due respect to Shakespeare, perhaps it is more to the point to keep in mind that he that filches from me my good name robs me of my credit status and makes me poor indeed.

6. Property Rights and Obligations

LOVE, romance, and tenure can help in determining whether a relationship is "shacking up" or consortium. But nothing does more to clarify the depth of feeling, the desire to stay together, the extent of commitment, than the way you handle your money.

How did Marcia feel about consortium? "I was always embarrassed about the money. If I did the shopping, George thought I spent too much. I hated to ask him for a share of what I spent." Now Marcia and George are married and "we don't worry about whose money is whose, or who bought what. Everything I have is his and vice versa."

Married couples, except for a little holding out, usually put the cash and property in a common pot. Divorce courts are available to married couples to decide the split at the end. Most single couples handle their money separately, each has his own savings and checking accounts; each owns his own stock and bonds, they rarely own a house together. But there is no reason for consorting couples to avoid these joint ventures. Marriage has certain built-in property rights, but consorts can create those rights in each other if they choose to. They don't often choose to.

The purpose here is to outline and describe property rights, to see which of them require the existence of marriage and which of them do not, and to explore means of holding property during consortium and division of property when consortium ends.

The status of marriage allows the husband and wife to charge their family-type expenses or "necessaries" to each other's accounts. This means that a wife can charge groceries and the grocer can collect from either the husband or the wife, whichever the grocer chooses. The husband can charge his clothing and the tailor can sue the wife to collect the bill. The right exists in the creditor to rely on the credit of either spouse to collect for basic family-type expenses. Let me repeat, this right is a *creditor's* right.

For example, a department store opens a charge account for Mr. Debtor. He uses the account to buy a television set for himself, his wife, and their kids, and then forgets to pay for it. The store credit manager can sue Mr. Debtor *or* Mrs. Debtor or both of them. The store credit manager doesn't choose to sue Mr. D. because he is the traditional breadwinner, nor does he refuse to sue Mrs. D. because she is the traditional homemaker. The credit manager is far more practical than that. He goes out to collect against the spouse with the money and he couldn't care less about traditional role-playing, women's liberation, or gallantry to the gentle sex. Therefore, the right of one spouse to charge necessaries to the other's account is a boon to the collection agency.

Family expense laws are predicated on the marriage relationship but lawful matrimony is not always required. If a couple holds itself out as married, one of the pair cannot duck his financial obligation by simply claiming on the courthouse steps that they are not married at all. Mr. and Mrs. A. lived together, called each other "Mr. and Mrs." and in all respects were married except that they neither went through the ceremony nor lived in a common-law marriage state. Mrs. A. was a homemaker, Mr. A. worked. T., the merchant, knew both Mr. and Mrs. A., and one day Mrs. A. bought a new set of dishes, pots, and pans from T. When T. wasn't paid, he sued Mr. A. because he had the money, and Mr. A. said, "Wait a minute, I'm not responsible for Mrs. A.'s debts. We aren't married." The judge said, "Right, you are *not* married; wrong, you owe T. the money." T. had been misled into relying on both Mr. and Mrs.

A., and he had a right to rely on both of them because of the way they conducted themselves.

Assuming, however, that in a consortium you are maintaining your own separate identities and independent credit, you are each responsible for your own purchases and debts. Let's also assume that though you are opting for consortium, you *want* to allow your partner to buy family-type expense items on your credit. It's easy (even easier than getting married). Credit managers are satisfied to have a charge account in the name of one solvent debtor. They are overjoyed and delighted to have two debtors to sue. Banks are pleased to have *anyone*, spouse or stranger, guarantee the loans they make. But before signing that guarantee, think twice. Long after the romantic haze has lifted, long after she has moved to a separate apartment, her default can bring the bank to the doorstep of her guarantor.

There was a time when certain of the conservative credit institutions would deny credit to a married woman, even one who was employed in a lucrative position. Women reported that their charge accounts were canceled when they got married, never to be reinstated when they were divorced. Married couples relying on two incomes to purchase a home were denied mortgages when the bank discounted or wholly ignored the wife's earning contribution. Horror stories of this kind were rampant and, after a struggle, reached Congress. At last, in October 1975, the Equal Credit Opportunity Act went into effect. The act condemns (*and* punishes) lending institutions that discriminate against a loan applicant "on the basis of sex or marital status."

Congress obviously intended to protect the married woman, but the law may protect consorts, too. Behind the white marble pillars of the great banks, little people sit in judgment on credit applications. Such applications from consorts may cause them to adjust their foulard neckties, swivel in their chairs, and resoundingly deny consorts the mortgage they want. The Equal Credit Opportunity Act is too new to have withstood the court test, but if it punishes discrimination in credit "on the basis of sex or marital status" shouldn't that help the consorts as well as married women?

Let's assume you have the cash or have the credit, and let's assume your consortium has deepened to the extent of your actually committing to joint investment. There are a number of ways people can own property, whether they are married or single. The ownership of property is defined by the state of the "title." Most of the things which you own do not have formal title documents and yet you own them; that means title is in your name. For example, when a hungry shopper passes through the check-out line with a cart loaded with goodies, they are toted up by the cashier, bagged by the teenager, and paid for. Title then passes from the store to the shopper. Generally the title to a minor purchase passes with the possession of the item. The major investments we make do not pass title with possession.

When a person, bullish on America, buys a part of a corporation, he doesn't put down his money and take with him the nuts and bolts in the factory. Instead he lays out his money for a piece of paper with a fancy embossed border, the stock certificate. That certificate evidences his share of ownership in the corporation. Driving an automobile does not make it your own, as Messrs. Hertz and Avis will assure you. Living in a house does not mean you can sell it and pocket the proceeds. In medieval England, before the days of county recorders of deeds, the sale and purchase of real estate was memorialized by a meeting of the townsfolk. They would witness an event called "Livery of Seizin." That is, the seller would hand over a clump of dirt to the buyer and everyone would watch and remember and title would pass. If you've witnessed a real-estate closing, you no doubt see the similarity. But now we rely on titles, pieces of paper instead of clumps of dirt, recorded in the public office rather than passed in the view of the neighborhood. Today, for major investments, title apart from possession determines ownership.

There are three major ways to hold title. The first, and typical consort method, is in your name alone. The second is joint tenancy and the last is tenancy in common. Both joint tenancy and tenancy in common are means of providing joint owner-ship and have nothing to do with marriage. Single people, con-sorts, lovers, business partners, and even married couples can own property in joint tenancy or tenancy in common, as they choose. Joint ownership, whether joint tenancy or tenancy in common, means that two or more persons own a share in the entire property. That is, if there are three joint owners, they each own a one-third interest in the property they purchase, and although each has a one-third interest, it is an *undivided* one-third. If they own a house, one doesn't own the attic, one the basement, and one the main floor. They each own one-third of the entire house. The only way to divide it is, after it's sold and paid for, to divide the pot (after the title companies, bro-kers, and lawyers take their share).

Joint tenancy is joint ownership with the right of survivor-ship. That means that if there are two joint tenants and one joint tenant dies, the surviving joint tenant automatically gets the whole. If there are more than two joint tenants, then the survivors still get the share of the first to die until the longest-living joint tenant gets it all.

Tenancy in common is joint ownership without the right of survivorship. While tenancy in common will provide consorts with an undivided one-half ownership in the house, the house remains in their separate estates when they die. For example, if consorts Jack and Jill buy a house on the hill in joint tenancy and Jill dies, Jack gets it all. If Jack and Jill own the house in tenancy in common and Jill dies, he gets to share it with Jill's mother (or whoever else inherits from her). That's a chilling thought, isn't it? And keep in mind that property acquired in joint tenancy can be converted to tenancy in common by one of the partners without the consent of the other — and sometimes in secret. One of the joint tenants deeds his undivided one-half share to a third person, a straw man, who then deeds the property right back to him. The gambit splits the joint tenancy and leaves the partners in ownership as tenants in common. The proposal of joint ownership of the home, the stock, and the car may be the true test of the strength of the consortium. There's no doubt that it's easier to rent, but if both buy, if both save to buy and both plunk down their savings, joint ownership is the only practical insurance that each can get back his own investment when the consortium is over. After all, when you both hate each other, you can both sell and split the cash or perhaps you can contract in advance to buy each other out.

If you simply cannot agree on what to do with the condominium when the love is gone, there is always the legal proceeding to force a split. This escape-hatch proceeding is called "partition." Partition is a kind of lawsuit by one joint owner against the other. The court hears evidence about the property itself, and decides whether it can be split into separate parcels among the joint owners and whether one put more money or effort into the property and is entitled to a larger share, and finally, if the property cannot be split, the judge orders the property placed for sale. Anyone can bid; the highest bidder gets the title; the cash, *after* the court costs and legal fees, is divided among the joint owners.

Partition, like joint tenancy and tenancy in common, is available to *anyone*, married persons or consorts. But this is not to say that every right that comes with the property ownership accrues to consorts as it does to the lawfully wedded. There are also the matters of dower, homestead, and community property.

Dower is the right created at early common law, and still existing in the statutes of many states, which insures that one spouse cannot be entirely disinherited by the other spouse. At early common law, wives had a *dower* interest in their husband's estates and husbands had a similar right called *curtesy*. Now the rights are all called dower and are basically the same for husband and wife, widower and widow. Even if the husband, for example, duly executes a legal and binding will which disburses his property among everyone but his wife, the dower laws will assure her that every beneficiary's share will diminish to the extent needed to assure her dower right — usually about one-third of the estate.

But there is no dower to the consort! In fact, Mrs. L., who claimed to be a widow entitled to dower, had to fight her case all the way to the United States Supreme Court to prove that before he died she and L. were lawfully married and therefore that she was entitled to a share in his estate, even though L. carefully planned to cut her out. If she had not proved her lawful *marriage*, she would not have inherited a dime.

Homestead statutes protect a portion of the family house, the homestead, from the claims of creditors. Each state has its own version of the homestead statute, but most say that a head of family has a sum, say $10,000, invested in his home which no creditors can touch even if they can attach or lien or garnish every penny he has, every thread of clothing, every morsel of food. While few would quarrel with the theory that everyone's entitled to a nest egg that is hands-off to creditors, the homestead laws have some serious flaws. In the first place, lowly apartment renters get no such break. In the second place, married women are not entitled to the homestead exemption unless their husbands are dependent, clearly departed, as in death, or just plain departed as in divorce. In the third place — and this is where consorts come in — single people are not considered heads of households or head of the family or anything else for homestead purposes. They get no homestead exemption. A Tennessee man who found himself in financial trouble claimed his homestead exemption to protect some of the equity in his farm. He failed when the court learned that the only occupants of the farmhouse were the bachelor and his nineteen-year-old male consort. The judge said that the purpose of homestead laws is to protect the family home, and where there is no family there is no right to such for the homestead laws.

Community property comes to us from the Spanish civil law. While most of our law derives from English common law, those states with Spanish-style architecture, Spanish-style street names, and Spanish-style sunshine have the residuum of Spanish law. Community property provides that assets acquired by a spouse during a marriage become the property of the "marital community." When the marriage ends the courts decide what property is community property and, having decided that, divide it up. The rationale of the community property law seems to be that the property acquired during a marriage comes of the joint efforts of the partners to it. Even if only one is the breadwinner, the other nonetheless contributes to its acquisition by industry and frugality.

Case after case holds that community property exists only in a marriage or at the very least when the parties believe *in good faith* that they have a valid, lawful marriage. Time and again community property has been held not to exist where the parties knowingly live together in, as the courts have said, "a meretricious or sinful relationship." Community property can only come into being in marriage, and no marriage equals no community. Consorts living in states that have the doctrine of community property were certain that each had his own property and neither had any claim to the property of the other. And then came the California Supreme Court case of Paul and Janet. Paul and Janet lived together for years, both of them knowing full well that they were not married. In fact they often discussed the possibility of getting married "for the children" but didn't. They bought a home, borrowed money, shared his name, obtained credit, told people they were married and had four children. Janet fulfilled the traditional role of homemaker and mother, and Paul did the husband-father bit. And then in 1971 Paul decided to leave Janet, and the fight over who got what began. Janet claimed that she was entitled to a community property split. Paul argued that everything was his, he worked for it, he owned it, and he cited an impressive list of case citations supporting his position: no marriage, no community property. But Janet fought on, right to the state supreme court, which held, in a most unusual decision, that since fault was no longer allowed to be considered in division of property in the divorce laws in California, the fact that both Paul and Janet were at fault and "living in sin" shouldn't affect their right to community property. Janet got her share. This may be the first case of divorce without marriage and the first case of community property between single people. This case presents a shaky precedent and others should not rely on it. The myriad of cases on the books would have left Paul and Janet as they were found: each with whatever property he or she had title to and the right to partition it, and Janet having the right to press a paternity suit for the support of the four kids.

Paul and Janet aside, the law generally provides no alimony, no separate maintenance, no homestead, no dower, no community property to the single couple. Harvey and Caroline's case in the Supreme Court in Washington illustrates the usual financial arrangement in consortium and what the law does or, more properly, does *not* do. When Harvey and Caroline got together, he had a good job and she had nothing but a beat-up Plymouth. They embarked upon a consortium with Harvey bringing home the salary and Caroline taking care of the household. As they saved, Caroline bought government bonds, sometimes with title as tenants in common with Harvey, often in her own name. Harvey paid little attention to the investments. And when Caroline bought a house in her own name, he approved. They lived together, they loved each other, they *trusted* each other. After many years, Caroline died. Suddenly, Harvey was surrounded by Caroline's long-lost relatives who claimed every dime of the property in Caroline's name. The judge said that Harvey had none of the rights protecting surviving spouses, was a stranger to Caroline as far as inheritance went, and that he must have intended a gift to Caroline to do with as she chose. She died without a will protecting Harvey, and the property passed to her relatives.

If you are set on buying things together, then you should think beyond the end of the consortium, till death do you part or till the day you walk out. Is it callous to plan for the day when you leave each other? Is it coldly businesslike to enter into a buy-sell agreement, options to purchase, decisions as to joint ownership with a view to the future? Well, maybe. But perhaps the most chilling, isolating, and transient of the consortiums are reflected in my interview notes.

"I've never been happier. I know he feels that way too. We don't doubt our love. It is deeper every day. We don't need a marriage license, it's only a piece of paper. Our relationship is solid as the Bank of England."

"By the way," I interpose, "how do you manage your savings?"

"We each have our own account."

"What about checking accounts?"

"He has his, I have mine."

"Do you own stock?"

"I don't, he does."

"Is he the beneficiary of your profit-sharing?"

"No, my parents are."

"Do you plan to buy a house or condominium?"

"Someday, if we ever get married."

7. Insurance

INSURANCE SALESMEN must stay up nights memorizing their company's version of the "rainy day" or "God forbid" speech. Indeed, no insurance companies could exist if it weren't for our lurking fear that, God forbid, something might happen and we should set aside a little something for a rainy day. Newlyweds change their addresses, change their names, and change their insurance beneficiaries. Consorts rarely bother, but consorts must also fear that, God forbid, they will have a rainy day too. So let's take a look at losses and damage and exclusions and liabilities, accident, fire, theft, invasion, plague, holocaust, and indemnity — the wonderful world of insurance.

Insurance policies are, first and foremost, contracts. They are simply documents which provide that if the insured represents his health, accident record, or personal status truthfully and pays the premium figured by the company on the basis of the representations, the insurer will pay him if, God forbid, he suffers an insured loss. Insurance companies are chartered by the states and regulated by acts of the federal and state legislatures, but, fundamentally, they are entering into individual contracts with each insured. This means that when you are contracting for insurance (and not just when you are making a claim on your insurance) you should boil up a vat of *strong* coffee and *read* the policy.

Insurers, like the rest of us, watch television programs where the suave felon carries out the ingenious plot to murder the heavily insured victim. In the attempt to stem crime and keep their insured alive (and thus avoid paying out) insurers want to be sure that beneficiaries love, or at least deeply care about, the insured. A policy owner must have "an insurable interest." The requisite insurable interest prevents you from taking out life insurance on the life, for example, of your landlord. You might be tempted to polish him off for the proceeds. Moreover, the staid insurers are not, like Jimmy the Greek, taking bets on who will make it. Think of the potential for gambling on the life of Fidel Castro. Should you pay a premium against a big recovery if he's assassinated? The companies refuse to write the policy. You do not have an insurable interest. All of this indicates that rarely, if ever, will an insurance company allow one consort to insure the life of the other. To these companies known for their conservatism, consorts have no "interest" in each other; husbands and wives do, lovers do not. Moreover, insurable interest may prevent one consort from owning his own insurance on his own life naming his consort as beneficiary on his death. She may, the insurance companies say, murder him for the proceeds and unless a television-smart detective uncovers the plot, she may succeed in collecting.

Andrew was, in fact, insured on his own policy when he was killed by gunshot wounds. His policy named "Mattie, my wife," as his beneficiary. But when Mattie came to collect, the insurance company refused to pay her. There was no question that she was entirely blameless in the murder, but both the company and Andrew's relatives argued that Mattie did not have an insurable interest. You see, she was not Andrew's wife but his consort. The court said that even though Mattie was innocent of the crime, she and Andrew had "meretricious relations" and "it is a matter of common knowledge that the practice of such relations often results in a fertile field for the breeding of violence which too frequently ends in the wanton destruction of human life." Mattie was left with neither Andrew nor his money. Even if Mattie had been held to have an insurable interest because of her long-standing relationship with Andrew, she might have been denied the proceeds because of Andrew's "fraud" in identifying her to the insurance company as his "wife."

Insurers are sticklers for the truth on the forms you complete when you take out the policy. One can appreciate their concern with a life insured's claims as to the state of his health. The ranks of actuaries and statisticians playing the numbers game at insurance companies also have presumptions of longevity based on the life we lead. Married men live longer than single men, they tell us. Consorts fall in the latter category according to the life underwriters interviewed. The higher the risk, the greater the premium, and to them consortium was risky business to life and health.

Tobias was issued a life insurance policy naming "Ada, my wife," as his beneficiary. Only three months later, he died, leaving Ada — his consort, *not* his wife — and Nina — his real, living wife and thus his lawful heir. Nina and Ada, consistent with the feelings they felt for each other, went to war over Tobias's insurance. The court was not so much concerned with the question of whether Ada had an insurable interest, but rather with the fact that Tobias had misrepresented himself on the insurance application. He had identified Ada as his wife *and* he had certified to being "correct and temperate in my habits." The judge said that it is fair to assume that if Tobias had disclosed that Ada was not in fact his wife, the company would have declined to issue the policy. "Tobias was living in an open state of adultery with Ada, which under the law made him guilty of a crime. He was therefore guilty of disreputable and unlawful conduct when he falsely certified that he was correct and temperate in his habits." Nina got nothing. Ada got nothing. Because Tobias had defrauded the company, it was freed from any obligation to pay.

The point of the cases, then, is to shop until you find an insurance company that will insure you for the benefit of your consort and apply honestly. The problem, of course, is obvious. There may be no such companies around. That is an even more serious problem for homosexual consortiums. The insurance companies pretend homosexuality does not exist. It should be noted, though, that insurable interest exists, if not in consortium then in business partnerships, in situations where the insured owes a financial debt to the beneficiary, and in various relationships where there is a joint ownership of property. If you cannot get insurance as consorts, but if a genuine financial relationship exists, you might obtain insurance on the basis of your financial relationship. For example, insurers issue "key man" insurance to protect a business venture from the loss of a working partner. Insurers protect creditors from the death of their debtor before a loan is repaid.

Not only do consorts have problems with insurance but bastards have fared poorly here too. In order for bastards to have an "insurable interest" in the life of their father, they must often show that he acknowledged them and that they relied on him, at least in part, for support.

In addition to protecting the lives of the insured, policies also protect against theft, loss, and damage to personal property. There are all kinds of policies for homeowners, apartment renters, and automobile drivers, among others. These insurance policies often have "omnibus clauses" that protect not only an insured, but "residents of the household." Unfortunately for consortiums, that phrase has been interpreted to mean "members of the insured's family." Medical and hospitalization insurance are for the insured and *spouse* and the *dependent* children of the insured. No marriage, no coverage. Some state legislatures are concerned about spouses, especially housewives, who lose their husband's medical insurance on divorce and then may be too old or unhealthy to have their own medical insurance. They are passing new laws preventing insurance companies from canceling a spouse because she is divorced from their insured. A laudable effort, but no help at all to consorts, who are not part of the "family" coverage in the first place.

Tina and Larry own a business together and had been consorts for several years. They're married now and there was a reason. Tina said she needed to know that Larry was permanently hers and that she wouldn't be moving on again as she had before she met him. Larry said he married her because that is what Tina wanted and anyway just living together was a hassle.

"We were living together for months, and I was paying premiums for all that time on the apartment and clothes and so forth. We were robbed. I called my insurance man. We argued and fought, but that son of a bitch wouldn't pay for Tina's stolen jewelry. He said, 'The company will pay for you, Larry, but it's not going to pay for the tramp you live with.' "

An insurance salesman who heard about Larry's experience was sympathetic. I knew he would be.

"The insurance salesman is a jerk and Larry didn't help. Why did they have to tell the company they were living together? Why didn't he just tell them the value of what he lost, collect for himself, and then give the girl her share?"

"You mean they'd have to lie?"

"Well . . ."

"That's fraud, that's a crime. Larry did the right thing and he was penalized."

"Yeah, well . . . you have to understand insurance. The companies are conservative."

Find an insurance company that will cover you, as you are, in truth. If not, save up your money in a sock, in case, God forbid, there's a rainy day.

8. Social Security

CHARLIE HAD just left the putting green and was enjoying the light afternoon breeze. Nettie sat down near him on the pastel-painted bench. Before long they had struck up a conversation. Nettie admired Charlie's courtly manners and he was attracted to her trim figure and blue hair. Day after day they met. They shared stories from the television news programs, showed each other wallet-sized pictures of their grandchildren's graduations and weddings. Nettie commiserated on Charlie's arthritis; he lent his arm to steady her during their strolls. Both were widowed, both were lonely, both were receiving social security, both were practical where money was concerned. They had to be.

Charlie, eighty, was receiving a monthly social security pension of about $275. Nettie, just seventy-six, was a widow, relying on her widow's social security pension of about $225. Today Charlie and Nettie are, among a growing mass of senior citizens, living in sin. They share their apartment, they share their lives, and they share their bed. Their children would disapprove if they knew, but they rarely visit and so Charlie and Nettie haven't bothered to tell them. As consorts, they share their total monthly social security of $500. If they married, Nettie would receive the higher of either half of her widow's benefits or half of Charlie's benefits and they would live on about $400 a month. Crime pays.

Bertha, not realizing the adverse economic effect of remarrying after her husband's death, married William. After all, Bertha was in love, and she didn't wonder why William's first wife had left him. The couple settled down in Kansas. Both

Bertha and William were past retirement age and, except for a few knickknacks, a couple of series E bonds, and their unwavering faith that they would win the state lottery, they relied for sustenance on their social security. Very soon, in fact on the day the social security check came in the mail, they realized their mistake. They barely managed on their reduced stipend, and while their love continued strong over the following years, it was gravely tested. They couldn't go to the movies; they never ate in a restaurant.

Then one bright day William's first wife called. She learned he had "married" Bertha. She was shocked and said she intended to divorce him. For all those years he had believed they were divorced, and now he learned he was a bigamist! When William broke the news to Bertha he waited for her tears. There were none. Bertha was delighted. She promptly filed an annulment suit to officially void her purported "marriage," the court promptly declared the marriage null and void, and Bertha filed a claim to reinstate her full widow's social security. Of course she and William continued to live together after the annulment and after his first wife did divorce him. As in the past, when they had believed themselves married, they carried on like married people. But that is where Bertha made her second mistake. The Social Security Administration refused to reinstate her widow's allotment. If she wasn't ceremonially married to William, she was now William's common-law wife in a state which recognized common-law marriage. Bertha stubbornly pursued her case to the United States Court of Appeals, but she lost her widow's rights.

It shoud be noted that, in order for Bertha or Nettie or anyone else to claim the widow's social security benefits in the first place, they had better be widowed from a real, old-fashioned marriage. Moreover the social security laws require that the couple be married for "not less than nine months" before the husband died. Jose and Petra were from Mexico and could not read or speak English. They believed that when they obtained their marriage license they were husband and wife. They obtained a license in 1960, went on their honeymoon, and set up housekeeping. In 1968, Jose became ill, and in deference to their religion they had a church wedding. A few weeks later Jose died, and when Petra applied for her widow's benefits, she had her mightiest English lesson. The state in which they lived did not recognize common-law marriage, and their ceremonial marriage had lasted less than the required nine months. No social security payments were allowed.

Nor did the widow P receive her social security benefits when she and P divorced after eighteen years of marriage and then resumed living together for thirty-five years more, without bothering to remarry. When P died, his "wife" was not his widow. Similarly, Lelia was left out in the cold. Lelia and Walter were consorts for ten years. Walter walked out and a few days later married Maggie. Realizing that he loved Lelia, he returned to her and they resumed their consortium. He never bothered divorcing Maggie, so that when he died it was Maggie, not Lelia, who picked up the social security.

If consorts have their problems with social security, it's obvious that bastards, who are in perpetual difficulty, have their problems here too. The Social Security Act has many provisions for allotments to children of deceased workers, but for the lowly bastard to share in these benefits he must prove (1) that the deceased worker was decreed in court to be his father, *or* in writing acknowledged him to be his child, *or* was ordered by a court to provide for him, *or* was actually proven to be his biological father; *and* (2) that the worker was living with his bastard at the time he died, *or* that the worker was contributing to his bastard's support at the time he died; *and* (3) to add to the difficulties, is the somewhat ambiguous requirement that under the laws of the state in which they resided, the bastard would be entitled to a share of the worker's property by inheritance.

Gregg and Lauri were high school students when they had sexual relations and Gregg, Jr., was born. There was never any question that Gregg, Jr., was his father's biological son, but he and Lauri never married, and as soon as he was out of high school Gregg went into the army and was shipped to Vietnam. Since the father was only a kid himself, he never provided any genuine support and Lauri relied on her parents' finances. Gregg contributed a few dollars and some baby clothes and toys. When he got to Vietnam, Gregg applied for a child's military allotment for his son, but before the red tape was cut and the application processed, Gregg was killed in action. Lauri applied for children's benefits for Gregg, Jr. The federal court found that the deceased worker had neither lived with the bastard nor contributed to his support. Benefits were denied.

Doc and Bessie lived together and had three children. Doc lived with his consort and their children until he died, but the kids were denied social security benefits because they lived in a state which disinherited bastards. The rights of children born during marriages contrast sharply with those born of consortium in many areas. Under the social security laws, the breach can be enormous. Fred and Jeanette married in 1960. Within five months they separated and Fred sued for divorce. In November 1962, before the divorce was granted, Jeanette gave birth to Tammie. Jeanette claimed that Fred was Tammie's father in that they had had sexual relations twice after the separation. Fred argued that he couldn't possibly be Tammie's father because in 1950 he had undergone a vasectomy. His doctor testified that vasectomies are about 99 percent effective in accomplishing sterility. The court held that since the operation was not 100 percent effective and since children conceived during lawful marriages are presumed to be legitimate, Tammie was his natural child. Shortly after the divorce Fred died, leaving Tammie a legitimate child fully entitled to all social security benefits.

You just can't beat the system, unless, like Charlie and Nettie, you are members of the swinging golden-age set.

9. Pensions and Death Benefits

IT SEEMS to be a basic right that anyone of sound mind and memory should be able to dispose of his property by will just as he chooses. Most states accept this premise, but not all.

In Louisiana, for example, fathers and mothers are prohibited from disposing of property to bastards beyond what is absolutely necessary to their sustenance. In South Carolina, a person with a lawful spouse and legitimate children cannot bequeath more than one-quarter of his estate to his illegitimate children and "paramour." Sam's will divided his property among "his wife, Grace," and "his children, Julia Mae, John, James, Corine, Boyd, George, and David." When he died, "his wife, Lula" and "his son, Henry" filed their objections to the will under the South Carolina statute. The judge decided that Grace was not Sam's lawful wife "but a woman with whom he lived in adultery" and that the seven children were bastards. The judge ordered three-fourths of the estate to Lula and Henry and only one-fourth of Sam's property to his paramour and their children.

In addition to the Louisiana limitation on bequests to bastards, Louisiana has community property. When Eugene left property acquired during his marriage to Mary to his bastard child, the court allowed a partial gift, but that gift came only from Eugene's half of the community property. Half of the property vested automatically in his widow. In another case, Leah died some time after the death of her legitimate daughter, Melanie. Melanie had five children, two of them illegitimate. When their grandmother Leah died, her will favored her daughter's two bastard children. Under the Louisiana statutes, the will was set aside and the three legitimate children received their grandmother's entire estate.

Except for a very few states, though, the general principles are that a person can leave his property to whomever he wishes. That is the law in most states and it is the law in New York where the saga of Edith and Joseph took place. Edith accused Joseph of rape in a criminal trial. Joseph was acquitted. Shortly after he was found not guilty, Edith moved in with Joseph and they lived together for many years. Edith had a daughter from a prior marriage; Joseph had a son Willie from his prior marriage. Years passed and Joseph, who had acquired a substantial estate in cash and farmland, was tending toward senility. He was planning his estate and told his son that he would leave his estate to him. Then, lo and behold, Edith went to Joseph, and accused Willie of raping her daughter. The girl concurred in the story. Incensed at his son, and forgetting that many years before Edith had made the same charge against him, Joseph changed his will in favor of Edith and her daughter and died. When Willie contested the will, the court said that Joseph could leave his property to anyone he wished.

In an Arkansas case, the brothers of Pink Jones wanted to set aside his will that left everything to "his wife, Lenora." Pink's brothers claimed that since Lenora was not a wife but a consort, the estate should go to them. Pink Jones's wishes were fulfilled, though, when the court agreed that he could leave his property to whomever he wished, even if the object of his gift was neither virtuous nor meritorious.

In order to accord full weight to laws like Louisiana's we should understand that those laws not only restrict the extent of gifts to consorts or bastards by will. There are also statutes restricting gifts to such donees which are *inter vivos* (during life) and *causa mortis* (shortly prior to death).

Jennie was certainly affected by these laws. Her consort gave her his entire estate in deeds during the last years of his life. All that remained passed to her under his will. She ended with only one-tenth of his property. The court set aside the will because Jennie was living in "open concubinage" with her consort and the effective statutes prevent persons living in open concubinage from receiving property given *inter vivos, causa mortis,* or by will. According to the judge (and this was a *recent* case) "the purpose of this provision is to protect the moral fabric of society against those who would brazenly flout its standards."

It is not only state laws which set out to punish consorts by limiting the give and take of their property, but private pension programs may do the same. Take a good look at the pension plan, retirement program, profit sharing, and insurance provisions which you are working for (and contributing to) on the job. You may learn, as did Abner's consort, that the boss makes certain moral decisions of his own. Abner was vice president of a bank when he died. Since his "widow" had not been his wife, she received none of his pension's death benefits. Pensions can limit beneficiaries as their terms provide and that often excludes consorts and bastards. What happened to the money in Abner's case? It stayed in the bank's hands, of course.

There are many more programs which contain retirement and death benefits. Under the Federal Death on the High Seas Act, children, whether legitimate or not, are beneficiaries. Under the Federal Employers' Liability Act, the government will pay bastards for the wrongful death of their federally employed parent.

Every state has some form of workmen's compensation statute. The laws allow an employee injured on premises either to sue his employer for negligence and get what the jury awards if the case is proven, or to elect to be compensated in the amount provided under the workmen's compensation provisions. If he chooses the workmen's compensation route, he needn't prove that it was his employer who was at fault, but he'll receive a fixed award that might be less than a jury would grant him. The purpose of these statutes is to relieve the injured employee from proving his case against the big, rich, well-represented employer. Workmen's compensation laws pay benefits to the injured employee, or, if he dies, to his dependents. Illegitimate children in the household of the deceased or receiving support from him have been held to be entitled to workmen's compensation benefits. One case went so far as to find that an illegitimate child born after her father's death on the job was dependent and entitled to funds under the statute.

In a Tennessee case, Ray lived with Thelma and her two children from a previous marriage. Ray had also been married and had a six-year-old son. When Ray died on the job, the court held that Ray's six-year-old had to share the workmen's compensation award with Thelma's two children. Even though the father of those children was alive and they had lived with Ray for only a year or so, the judge said that all three children became dependents of Ray before his death and for purposes of workmen's compensation that was all that mattered.

While children fare well under workmen's compensation law, consorts do not. The courts have held that persons claiming death benefits under those statutes must either be widows of a lawful marriage or dependent members of the family of the deceased. Consorts do not qualify under either definition. In a case denying workmen's compensation benefits to a consort, the decision of the court said: "The claimant is responsible for the illegal relation which she assumed and carried on with the deceased employee. There was no duty on his part to support or care for her. Either was at liberty to break off or terminate the relation at his or her own pleasure without any recourse whatever to the other . . . The statute will not be extended to bring within its folds those who voluntarily enter into a relation not countenanced by the law of this State."

The numerous private plans, government programs, and local laws providing for pensions and death benefits are all different. Reading all of them and interpreting all of their applications is virtually impossible, if not just deadly dull. But remember, you are paying for these benefits, whether in direct salary contribution, deduction from pay, taxes, or cost of goods and services. If you are into consortium until retirement or death, you ought to find out what you get for your money.

10. Taxes

CHIEF JUSTICE JOHN MARSHALL is credited by the historians with having great foresight. Perhaps he envisioned our present taxes and their effects on consortium when in 1819 he reflected "that the power to tax involves the power to destroy; that the power to destroy may defeat and render useless the power to create."

Everyone, married or single, who earns a minimum income must pay income tax. But married people have certain options open to them which may reduce their taxes. Consorts have no such option. Income taxes are, of course, on a graduated scale. That is, the more money one earns the higher bracket he is in, so the percentage of tax increases. Because of that graduated scale, those who earn high income are always trying to find ways to split their tax liability. For example, a wealthy woman penciled the words "in trust for my daughter" on the deed to an apartment building she owned. She paid tax on her other income and her daughter, in the lowest bracket, paid tax on the building's rental income — that is, until the Internal Revenue Service said the arrangement was a sham to split income. The woman was forced to pay the tax on the rents in her own high bracket. The only way she could accomplish an income split was by actually conveying the apartment building into her daughter's own name, and she wasn't about to do that.

The most common way to get the benefits of an income split is through the means Congress provided, the joint income tax return. But the joint income tax return is available to married people — not single people, not consorts. Lou learned this lesson when he got out of his marriage by a Mexican divorce and promptly "married" his girlfriend Linda. Lou's first (and only) wife had the divorce set aside because the Mexican courts lacked jurisdiction and the I.R.S. had Lou's joint tax return set aside because he filed it with Linda, who, being the second "wife" of a bigamous marriage, was no wife at all.

Married couples are not required by law to file joint income tax returns; they have a choice. They can file either jointly or separately, whichever saves them more tax money. So long as there's a substantial difference between the income of one tax-payer and the income of his spouse, the joint tax return generally saves, because, of course, it splits the higher income between two taxpayers and thus lowers the percentage taxed.

Married couples, however, do have one disadvantage that consorts do not. Married couples, whether they file jointly or separately, if they do not itemize their deductions, get only *one* standard deduction. Since the I.R.S. considers consorts single taxpayers, each gets his or her own standard deduction.

In dollars and cents, here's what this means. Let's assume that a *married* couple both work. She is a secretary earning $10,000 a year; he is a salesman earning $17,000 a year. They rent an apartment, have no unusual medical bills, charitable gifts, or interest payments, so they take the standard deduction rather than itemizing. Applying the Internal Revenue Code as it was in 1975 (but ignoring the special 1975 tax reduction act, which may or may not be in effect in future years), their federal income tax on a joint return comes to $5,500. If they had chosen to file separately (still getting only one standard deduction because they are married), their taxes would increase. He would pay $4,038 on his return, she would pay $1,700 on her return, making a higher total for the couple of $5,738.

But let's take the same couple with the same income and call them consorts. They are single and must file separate returns, but each gets his own standard deduction. The $17,000 a year consort pays $3,288 in federal income tax. The $10,000 a year consort pays $1,530 in federal income tax and the total federal tax obligation of the consortium is only $4,818. So, compliments of the Internal Revenue Service, the consortium has saved $682 that year in tax and is on its way to vacation in Florida.

The only way for you, with *your* income and *your* deductions, to figure out whether you're ahead of the tax game single or married is to sit down at tax time and work out some sample returns. Pretend you're married and figure up a joint return. Then do your own single returns and see who's ahead. If you find it's cheaper to file a joint return, well, you've learned something, but don't try it. Consorts attempting to file joint tax returns are violating the law and paying stiff penalties.

Not only are consorts denied the option of filing a joint income tax return, but efforts at dependency exemptions for dependent consorts have failed as well. Victor and Laura would have celebrated their silver wedding anniversary — if there had been a wedding. Their consortium followed the traditional roles, Victor the breadwinner, Laura the homemaker. At fifty-nine, Victor concluded that Laura was unable to provide her own support and, knowing that he couldn't file a joint tax return, he decided to try for the dependency credit, but the I.R.S. picked up the tax deficiency.

The I.R.S. and the Tax Court of the United States decided that Eddie went too far. He claimed Annie as his dependent common-law wife in 1949, Lulu as his common-law wife in 1950, and Harriet as his dependent *mother* in 1951. Eddie couldn't prove that any of them was a wife or mother and was ordered to pay up.

Those cases, Victor's and Eddie's, were decided under the 1939 Internal Revenue Code, which allowed dependency deductions only for a class of "dependent" relatives. A dependent has minimal income, or is a student, or is under nineteen years of age. Under the 1939 code, to take the dependent on your income tax return, that person had to be a son or daughter, a grandchild, a stepchild, a brother, sister, or "step-sibling," a parent or grandparent, an in-law, a niece or nephew, aunt or uncle.

But in 1954 the Internal Revenue Code was revised and the

definition of dependents broadened to include nonfamily members. The purpose of the expansion of the definition of dependents was *not* to help Victor and Eddie take their consorts as dependents, but, according to Congress, was to help people with foster children or children awaiting adoption by giving them the dependency deduction. Congress didn't limit its revision to foster children or children awaiting adoption, however; it expanded the dependent's definition to include *anyone* who lives with the taxpayer, in his household. Sure sounds as if consorts fit that definition.

Leon T. read the 1954 revision and, just as any good taxpayer would, found the loophole. Leon T. and Tina J. had lived together, with Tina totally dependent on Leon's income. In 1954, as soon as the revised code went into effect, Leon jumped at the chance to take Tina as a dependent. The judge deciding the I.R.S. case against Leon posed the question, "Is the language used in Section 152 (a) (9) of the Code to be construed literally so as to embrace an individual living in illicit intimacy with a taxpayer?" Not on your life, Leon. The judge decided that Congress never intended to cut the tax bill of a person maintaining "an illicit relationship in conscious violation of the criminal law," and Congress would never have intended "to countenance, if not to aid and encourage, a condition universally regarded as against good public morals." So, although the language of the code seems to include dependent consorts as tax exemption dependents, the I.R.S. and the courts have refused to give the statute a *literal* reading and allow the tax saving.

In another case, Alfred got the double whammie. When Judy's divorce was final, in 1962, she moved right in with Alfred and brought her two children along. Alfred and Judy got married in mid-1963. They could not file joint tax returns in 1962 and Alfred had *no* dependents in 1962. Moreover, in 1963, while Alfred provided some support for Judy's kids, he could not prove that he provided more support than their natural father and he got no deduction for them that year either.

If you think Alfred had problems, consider Daniel's case.

When Daniel and Willa became consorts, she brought her mother along. Mother lived with them and both she and Willa were dependent on Daniel for support. But when Daniel claimed both of them for dependency exemptions, the Internal Revenue Service sued him. Willa didn't qualify because she was an illicit consort. Her mother didn't qualify because she was not related to Daniel, but was part of the consortium.

An unmarried person who provides the support for others may qualify for the special lower tax rates provided for "head of household." These special rates reduce the percentage of income taxed by the federal government and result in real savings. But, in order to qualify, the head of household must maintain a home for any of a number of *relatives.* Consorts do not count.

If consortium costs money during a lifetime, the tax disadvantages at death are even more severe. Cash and property passing at death are taxed by both the federal government and the states as well. The Federal Estate Tax is a tax imposed on dying itself. Anyone who dies owning more than the exempt minimum has a federal tax imposed on his estate.

The federal government tried to treat every estate equally, so every taxpayer's estate had the same bite no matter where he died. But some states have community property laws based on the Spanish civil law heritage and most states, based on English common law, do not. In community property states, the cash and property acquired during marriage are treated as belonging to a common fund owned by husband and wife regardless of who actually went out of the home to work and brought it into the marriage. When one spouse dies in a community property state, only his one-half of the community is included in his estate and taxed. Federal Estate Tax, like income tax, is based on a bracket system. The more in your estate, the higher the percentage of tax. This meant that people from community property states would receive a substantial benefit over the deceased breadwinners in the other states, whose whole estate would be subject to estate tax.

In order to treat all of the dead taxpayers the same, Congress gave a "marital deduction" to people who died after having been domiciled in a non-community-property state. The "marital deduction" takes out of the taxable estate the share (up to one-half) which is inherited by a surviving spouse. In other words, the estate is split in half, just as it is automatically in community property states, and only one-half is taxed; since less cash and property pass, it passes at a lower bracket. The marital deduction results in a genuine tax break to the estate of the person who dies married. The consort gets no such benefit. Both community property and the marital deduction have the same requirement, *marriage*.

The death tax bite does not end with the federal government, because states have death taxes too. These are either like the Federal Estate Tax, with breaks for the married, or they are taxes not on the estate but on the beneficiary who receives the property. If you die in a state which taxes the beneficiary, the state looks at who the beneficiary is to determine how much tax he pays for the privilege of inheriting from you. Property passing to a surviving spouse gets a bigger exemption and a lower rate than property passing to a child of the deceased. Property passing to a child gets a bigger exemption and lower rate than property passing to a sister or brother of the deceased. And so forth. The lowest exemption and the highest tax are on property passing to strangers, and — you guessed it — consorts are considered strangers.

If you have the feeling that everyone is ganging up to make your consortium difficult and *expensive,* if you sense that those with the power to tax are also setting out to destroy your romantic idyll, well, you're probably not paranoid, you are probably correct.

11. Discrimination in Employment

IF YOU WANT to be President of the United States of America, you should not even consider consortium. Get married. If, however, your ambitions are less grand, consortium is probably not going to cause you a problem on the job. There are cases, though, of employment discrimination based upon "immorality." Often these involve the individual judgments of the boss or the personnel manager and do not rise to the dignity of company policy. Employees on "at will" jobs, those which can be terminated at the sole discretion of the boss, have little standing to complain and seldom have access to the courts. When "at will" employees are discharged because of something the company finds objectionable in their personal lives, the incident is lost in the personnel files.

Homosexuals definitely face employment discrimination, and for them job security often compels secrecy. Open consortium presents a tremendous risk. People who at initial interviews "seem to be homosexuals" may not be offered jobs, and since no explanation is given, they can only conjecture as to the reason. Homosexuals (or suspected homosexuals) may be terminated from "at will" positions without any chance to defend their right to employment. Even those who are employed in government or union positions which require a showing of "cause" for discharge are only rarely told that the actual cause for their dismissal is that they are believed to be homosexual. And employees who have been told that they are being discharged because they are believed to be homosexuals only rarely take action. The issue, of course, should not be whether the employee is or is not a homosexual, but whether, assuming that he is, his performance on the job will be adversely affected. Only a few have taken the issue on, but with the gay movement's efforts for frankness and for the preservation of the rights of homosexuals, cases of employment discrimination should soon be filling the courts.

Thus far the results of the cases have not been encouraging. A happily married man was discharged by the Federal Aviation Authority for having engaged in homosexual activity eight years earlier. The decision to terminate by the F.A.A. was backed by the Civil Service Commission and was upheld in the courts. The National Aeronautics and Space Administration (NASA) terminated an employee following his arrest for a minor traffic violation. The employee was in the automobile with a friend who admitted that some homosexual preludes were made. An investigation commenced and the employee admitted that he experienced homosexual desires. NASA discharged him immediately. The employee involved was a budget analyst for NASA. He argued that if he were a homosexual, it was a private matter and had nothing to do with his ability to analyze NASA's budget. It took years of litigation and the United States Court of Appeals to compel NASA to prove that the employee's efficiency in his job was adversely effected by the facts of his sexual history. Of course, NASA could prove nothing. Other courts have been less demanding on government employers. Take for example the judge who upheld dismissal of a homosexual because the homosexual "act" itself is "immoral, indecent, lewd and obscene."

Heterosexual consortium is only rarely used as a basis for dismissal, but it has been done. Neil M. was employed as a clerk with the United States Post Office in 1967, when he was told to appear for a Civil Service Commission interview. At the "interview" Neil was told that a secret investigation had been made which conclusively proved the most shocking immoral conduct! Was Neil stealing the social security checks? Was Neil helping the C.I.A. open the mail? No. Neil was living "with a young lady without the benefit of marriage." Neil's response was "Oh, sure." The United States Civil Service Commission fired him for "immoral conduct." It took until 1970 for the case to be decided by the United States District Court. There the judge held that the termination was arbitrary, capricious, and violative of a constitutional right to a private sex life. He endorsed Neil's argument that the most disturbing aspect of the case was the "spectre of the government dashing about" investigating Neil's private consortium.

The police commissioner of New York City charged police officer W.S. with "consorting with a woman, not his wife," to which W.S. pleaded guilty and for which he was discharged by the department. He was reinstated with back pay on appeal to the New York courts, which found that W.S.'s living arrangements were not "directly prejudicial to good order, efficiency, or discipline." (The judge also took the police commissioner to task for identifying the woman in the official specifications as a "Negress," holding that it was improper to designate her by race, religion, or descent. "Such conduct," said the judge, "must be challenged and condemned wherever it appears . . . it is invitation and encouragement to bigotry.")

In 1966, Eugene C., a tenured junior college professor, was discharged for immoral conduct. Patricia, a former student, moved in with him before she was divorced and stayed on after an invalid Mexican divorce decree. Before living with Patricia, Eugene C. lived with Frances. Before that, he was married to Barbara. He was dismissed for "immoral conduct." The state appeal court agreed with the school board because "the calling of a teacher is so intimate, its duties so delicate . . . The teacher's habits, his speech, his good name, his cleanliness, the wisdom and propriety of his unofficial utterances, his associations are all involved." Teachers have always had their problems with meeting the school board's amorphous requirement of "moral conduct." In one case, a local school board's dismissal of a teacher was upheld on the grounds that he had strolled the streets in the town caressing and fondling a store window mannequin. There seems to be a giant gap, though, between the type of dismissals prior to 1970 and those after 1970. For example, an admitted homosexual, active in gay organizations, retained his job as a school librarian at a midwest university in 1970. Probably he would have lost his job if the case had come up a few years earlier.

If consortium causes couples problems on the job, marriage is at least as damaging. Are you shocked? Well, the grand old institution of marriage is damned by the most conservative employers. They do not allow fellow employees to marry each other. Does this make sense? Is it just? Does it encourage consortium? You bet your life. In fact, even at companies who have no published nonmarriage policy it is often smart to be consorts or *pretend* not to be married. Once you announce the joyous news of your nuptials, the boss suspects a lack of dedication to the job, the bride's waistline is gazed upon in expectation of her expectation, and her salary increases start drifting into memory.

In 1975, however, the Supreme Court of Nebraska struck a blow *for* marriage. That time-honored tradition and status had been cause for dismissal in the personnel rules of a local government office in that state. The court held that the personnel rule which conditioned continued employment on city employees not marrying each other was unfair and contrary to the public policy encouraging marriage (and discouraging consortium). Marriage, the court said, is a right protected by the United States Constitution.

Be careful, though, before you buck the personnel rules at your plant. First, the rules relating to *government* employment are subject to safeguards often not available in private employment. Second, as long as employers believe that married women can be paid less than single women "because married women have a man to support them" (employers still cling to that notion, the Equal Rights Amendment notwithstanding), marriage may still be a disadvantage on the job.

We are in the midst of wild and wonderful changes in the law. The plight of the pregnant woman and employment discrimination is another area of change, but here the judges are bogged down in old-fashioned sentiments on motherhood and maternal roles. The changes are slow in coming.

The regulations of the United States Air Force stated that a woman would be terminated "with the least practicable delay" if she is a parent of a child under eighteen, hers or someone else's, living with her in her household for more than thirty days a year, or gives birth to a child. When it was at last decided that the regulation was discriminatory against women, the air force amended the regulation in 1971 to provide that a woman officer would be discharged permanently and "with the least practicable delay" when a medical officer determines that she is pregnant. When Mary G., a first lieutenant in the air force, became pregnant, she was discharged and her efforts to overturn the regulation in the courts failed.

Ms. Irene was a single schoolteacher in Alabama when rumors came to the attention of the county superintendent that Ms. Irene was pregnant. He took it upon himself to call on the local doctor who, ignoring the rights of his patients to the physician-patient privilege, told the superintendent that, yes, Ms. Irene was two months pregnant and considering an abortion. A hearing of the school board convened, and Ms. Irene was questioned:

"Q. Did you tell the Superintendent, in effect, that the doctor could not be correct that you were two months pregnant, because your fiancé had been gone four months?

"A. Right.

"Q. Did you mean by that that you had been having relations with your fiancé up until he left?

"A. I don't think that's . . ."

Ms. Irene's attorney: "Answer the question."

"A. Okay. Yes, I'm twenty-eight years old, and I don't think the Board or anybody else can tell me what I can do with my private life.

"Q. Then you do acknowledge that you had sexual relations

with this man while you were unmarried and while you were
teaching here?

"A. Sure.

"Q. Will you tell us where those relations took place?

"A. Well, I have never been inside of a hotel.

"Q. Where do you recall different times that it took place?

"A. Mostly in his car.

"Q. Have you also had relations with any other man?

"A. No."

The school board committee went into secret session and
then announced that it decided to discharge Ms. Irene, effective
immediately. The United States court ordered Ms. Irene reinstated. It was outraged that the evidence against her was from
an investigation into personal matters by interrogation of her
doctor. "If the right of privacy means anything," it said, quoting a Supreme Court decision on contraception, "it is the right
of the *individual,* married or single, to be free from unwarranted
governmental intrusion into matters so fundamental . . . as the
decision whether to bear or beget a child." One judge disagreed
and stated that if Ms. Irene had a constitutional right to privacy,
she waived it when her "morals became street talk in Glorada,"
the town in which she taught. "Rumor of immorality of a public
schoolteacher in a small town travels fast" said the judge in his
1974 dissenting opinion, urging that Ms. Irene be discharged
for the "immoral conduct" of having premarital sexual intercourse and a two-month pregnancy.

The Illinois courts also disagreed with the dissenting judge
when a teacher, eight and a half months pregnant and unmarried, was discharged. The judges said that for it to uphold a dismissal, the school board would have to prove that the teacher's
situation damaged the students. While the court did not strike
"immorality" as a cause for dismissal it required the board to
prove that the "immorality" caused harm to pupils, faculty, or
the school itself. "Where his professional achievement is un-
affected, where the school community is placed in no jeopardy,

a teacher's private acts are his own business and may not be the basis of discipline." If she were pregnant and married, her job would not have been threatened at all. Concluding that the board had no evidence whatever that the unwed pregnancy of Ms. K. caused any harm to anyone, she was reinstated.

Since we are unlikely ever to get a reliable definition of "immorality" it seems that the time has come to strike the phrase off the list of justifications for an employee's discharge. But the term still hangs on, and while the courts are compelling employers to prove that "immorality" adversely affects performance on the job, we'll probably never be able to quantify how "immorality" or consortium keeps an applicant from being hired in the first place, being promoted, or being discharged from private "at will" employment. I do believe, though, that candidates for the presidency in today's society should be advised to marry their consorts if they hope to be elected.

12. Military Service

If he had sung "Don't sit under the apple tree with anyone else but me till I come marching home" to his wife instead of his consort, he might have been able to stay home in the first place. The Selective Service Acts of the United States have always granted favored status to married men and especially married men with children. These deferments have not been available to consorts.

Under the latest voluntary army provisions, a volunteer may be single or married, a parent or not, but the draft provisions which still hang on authorize the President to prescribe rules which grant deferments to married draftees with dependent wives and children and even to draftees with wives who have no children, in hardship cases. These provisions still speak about *wives,* not consorts. Moreover the provisions specifically limit deferment to persons with wives and children "with whom they maintain a *bona fide* family relationship in their homes." What Congress is saying is that bastards don't qualify as your children unless you live with them.

But the military doesn't stop there. Once they have you in service, once they have you marching, saluting, eating powdered eggs, and shouldering a weapon, it continues to make it tough on consorts. In its new P.R. buildup the military has made a pitch about its great benefits over and above basic military pay. And the benefits *are* good. There are, for example, travel allowances, subsistence payments (the army's clever phrase for reimbursement for meals when there's no nearby "messing facility"), transportation arrangements, and housing allowances, and they are all compliments of Uncle Sam, all with love from the Pentagon, and all available to the member of the uniformed services and "his spouse" — *not* his consort.

Travel and meals and housing are only the beginning. For the person lucky enough to be a soldier on active duty, the benefits are nonstop. His wife also receives free medical and dental care. His widow receives all this too, but only as long as she is "un-remarried." So, while consortium doesn't pay during the soldier's life, "living in sin" with someone else entitles the widow to have her body treated and her teeth drilled compliments of the U.S. Government — until she remarries.

The military, in its wisdom, denied its servicemen's bastards any of the medical and dental benefits available to their legitimate children, reasoning that its soldiers would "shun illicit relations because their offspring may not one day reap the benefits of the Dependents' Medical Care Act. 10 U.S.C. §1071." That was the rationale and that was the law until 1972, when the bastard daughter of a fourteen-year-old mother and an army father brought suit against then Secretary of Defense Melvin Laird, claiming she was being discriminated against. The United States District Court agreed that there is "constitutional dignity in the right of illegitimate children to share equally with legitimate children in governmentally conferred benefits." The judge ruled that the Army's rationale that to deny dentistry would discourage service members from illicit sex was ridiculous, and held the discrimination unconstitutional.

The Pentagon's largesse does not stop with lifelong benefits. The Pentagon adds insurance to the benefits of a military career. Congress started providing insurance to the members of the armed services when it enacted the War Risk Insurance Act during World War I. That insurance paid a pension to widows of deceased soldiers, but the payments ended when a widow remarried *or* lived in "open and notorious illicit cohabitation with another." When Mr. Prince went off to make the world safe for democracy, his wife, Pearly, waited for him faithfully. Prince died in the war and Pearly started collecting her $57.50 a month under the War Risk Insurance Act until 1922, when the government notified her that she had forfeited her pension by her open and notorious illicit cohabitation with Holmes. Pearly objected, "Well, sure, I've had three illegitimate kids with Holmes, but we only had sex three times, once for each kid, and never lived together." Holmes was employed by a traveling circus. The judge didn't believe Pearly's version of the conception of her three children, he didn't believe that even a circus headliner could have the record Pearly claimed that Holmes established, and in those days, on the eve of the Roaring Twenties, the judge was not prepared to allow Pearly to receive government money and live so immorally.

The War Risk Insurance Act has long since been replaced by the National Service Life Insurance Act, which has no termination provisions for consortium, only for remarriage. Under the terms of National Service Life Insurance a widow of a man killed in service receives insurance payments as long as she is "unremarried." A widow had benefits reinstated when the Veterans Administration decided to cut off her payments because of her consortium. She was neither ceremonially wedded nor common-law married and so she was an "unremarried" widow. Consortium worked for her, but the story doesn't end with National Service Life Insurance.

Under the latest regulations, the military can refuse overseas assignments to anyone with a history of "moral turpitude including sexual perversion." Officers who are *married* are given preferred assignments for establishing a household — not so for consorts. Also, a *married* military couple may get special treatment as to concurrent tours of duty and assignments.

In 1973 the military regulations were revised to enforce a directive against "discrimination on basis of race, color, age, creed, national origin, political affiliation, sex or *marital status.*" It remains to be seen whether the brass will ban all discrimination based on sexual conduct (the suits filed by homosexual soldiers have not yet been decided) or nonmarital status. This is still the Army, Mr. Jones.

13. Immigration

IF the Statue of Liberty were to reflect the United States immigration, naturalization, and deportation laws, the words at her feet would have to be rewritten:

> *Give me your tired, your poor,*
> *Your huddled masses yearning to breathe free,*
> *The wretched refuse of your teeming shore . . .*
> *But as for your consort, your bastard, your homosexual,*
> *your "immoral," don't bother me . . .*

Immigration to the United States is severely limited and visas often depend on relationships — the married kind, not consortium. Spouses and legitimate children receive visas to join their mates or parents in the United States. Illegitimate children receive visas through their mothers only.

According to the statutes, aliens are excluded from the United States if they are, among other things, "afflicted with psychopathic personalities or sexual deviation," or if they have been involved in a "crime involving moral turpitude." Among those excluded from our streets are prostitutes, pimps, and "aliens coming to the United States to engage in any immoral sexual act."

Once here, aliens are subject to deportation. A simple consortium arrangement may carry this price tag. Inger, a Danish citizen, came to the United States and settled in Los Angeles. There she met a married man and started having an affair with him. Naturally, since he already had a wife, Inger didn't move in with her lover and she kept her job. Theirs was a strictly "working late at the office" relationship. When the husband had the opportunity to attend a convention in Vienna, he left his wife at home and took Inger with him. Inger visited her family in Copenhagen, the couple rendezvoused in Paris, and back they came. They returned first to Vancouver and then arrived in Seattle, where they registered in a hotel as "Mr. and Mrs." But who greeted them at the hotel? Who broke into a rage? Who screamed threats and recriminations? No, not the wronged wife, but the immigration officers she had obviously tipped off. Armed with the tawdry story of romance in Paris, the immigration official ordered Inger deported. The United States District Court agreed that anyone guilty of such moral turpitude should not be allowed to live in Los Angeles. The United States Court of Appeals agreed that Inger should be packed off to Denmark. But armed with justice on the one hand, and her lover's legal fees and court costs on the other, Inger managed to bring her case all the way to the United States Supreme Court. There it was decided, with only one dissenting vote, that Inger should be allowed to stay — not because the immigration law was unconstitutional, or unfair, or prudish, but because the law didn't apply to Inger. It is designed to exclude prostitutes or persons coming to our shores "with an immoral purpose." Inger's "purpose" was to reside in her own flat and keep her own job. What would have happened if Inger's relationship was a true consortium and she had chosen to fulfill the role of living with her consort and being supported by him? Goodbye, Inger.

Morocco-born David made the mistake of having sexual inter-course with a girl under eighteen. She was willing, but because she was under age her consent didn't count, and David was convicted of the crime of "statutory rape." David was sentenced to three years in prison and then deported, because he was "unfit," according to our immigration authorities, to remain in the United States, even though by the time he finished serving his sentence his girlfriend would have been of age.

After five years of continuous residence in the United States an alien may apply to become a naturalized citizen, *if* during all the time he has lived in this country he "is a person of good moral character, attached to the principles of the Constitution of the United States, and well disposed to the good order and happiness of the United States." Ducan was an alien happy to reside in the United States and overjoyed to have left his wife home in Zoblace, Yugoslavia. She was equally pleased that an ocean divided them. When Ducan met Rose, this nation looked better than ever. They fell in love and lived together in consortium. They had children and he finally obtained a divorce and Ducan and Rose married. Ducan studied his American history, memorized the Constitution, and applied for naturalization. His petition was refused because, the judge held, by living with another woman while he was married he had "committed morally reprehensible acts which debarred him from naturalization."

In another case, Maria of Czechoslovakia fared better. She and her consort had lived together for fifteen years before his divorce and five years after his divorce when they finally married. A few months after the wedding Maria applied to become a naturalized citizen. Naturally the immigration officials turned her down in their valid attempt to keep the United States safe from riff-raff. The judges of the Federal Appeals Court allowed Maria to become a citizen. In the first place, her lover was divorced for five years and so for those years Maria was not an adulteress, only a lover. In the second place, "a person may have a 'good moral character' though he has been delinquent on occasion." The judges refused to rule that consortium meets the test of "good moral character," but did decide that Maria was not so immoral that this country couldn't absorb her, since she had "only one lover and she had been true to him for over twenty years."

If the immigration officials had a setback because Maria became a citizen, that's nothing to the defeat they suffered in the spring of 1975. Until then, homosexuals were excluded from becoming naturalized citizens. Homosexuals have also been deported, the courts holding that they have "psychopathic personalities." And it mattered not that Supreme Court Justice Douglas said that "to label a group so large 'excludable aliens' would be tantamount to saying that if Sappho, Leonardo da Vinci, Michelangelo, André Gide and perhaps even Shakespeare were to come to life again they would be deemed unfit to visit our shores." It didn't matter that Justice Douglas made that eloquent argument, because he made it in a dissent. The majority just didn't agree with him. Then along came Paul, a New Zealander, a veteran of the United States Army — and what did he want? He wanted to become a citizen of the United States. But Paul was a homosexual. The immigration officials, predictably, turned him down. Unpredictably, Paul took an appeal. The question was whether a homosexual could meet the test of good moral character under the naturalization statute. The immigration bureaucrats said "No." The court said, "Why not?" The judge found Paul's conduct acceptable by ethical standards of 1975. His sexual conduct was no different from that of many other persons of his age, twenty-eight. He was not "sexually involved with minors." He did not "use threat or fraud." He did not "take or give money." He did not "engage in sexual activity in parks, theatres, or any public places." In fact, Paul's conduct was like anyone else's. It's just that his sexual partners, consenting adults in private, were men instead of women. Paul's petition for naturalization should be granted, the judge decided. "We'll appeal," said the Department of Justice.

And so, little by little, the law becomes more understanding and the Statue of Liberty more welcoming.

14. The Loose Ends

THIS BOOK started with the idea that marriage is and has been the elemental relationship. Subsequent chapters have attempted to cover the law that affects single people bucking this basic mode of life. Yet throughout our entire social and legal code, there is always still another nuance of law that assumes the existence of lawful matrimony. Here are odds and ends of a few more marriage-related laws.

A wife is not competent to testify against her husband and vice versa. The secrets of the marriage bed stay right there "to preserve marital harmony." And, in one case, the United States Supreme Court held that it was against the law to allow a wife to testify against her husband even though she volunteered her testimony. (She wanted to testify against him because he was charged with violating the Mann Act, taking the other woman across state lines for immoral purposes). The Supreme Court absolutely refused to allow the testimony because of the "marital privilege." But consorts have no such privilege. Their relationship is not one that the law seeks to preserve, so either consort can, voluntarily or under subpoena, speak out against the other.

Did you know that when one spouse goes into bankruptcy certain allowances, like widow's awards, and homestead are preserved to his spouse and *not* his consort?

In most states a person can be adjudicated mentally incompetent and confined to an institution with his spouse or relatives being notified and having a chance to defend him, but his consort may never even be told of the proceedings.

A person can produce 200 gallons of homemade wine without

paying any federal liquor tax if he registers with the federal government *and* is the head of the household producing wine for use by his family. Consorts pay the tax.

This list will go on and on as long as laws are on the books. Whether they be federal enactments or small-town ordinances, marriage runs through them.

15. A Contract for Living Together

SINCE this book has been dedicated to telling the truth, the whole truth, and nothing but, consortium has taken on an aura of great legal peril. Laws are not easily changed, but now that you've been warned you may be better able to cope with your lifestyle.

What follows is a "contract" for living together. It deals with many of the problems outlined in the foregoing chapters. But this "contract" is *not* a contract! A true contract is an agreement between parties that is *enforceable* in the courts. The "contract" which follows is intended to perpetuate consortium; it is therefore in derogation of the public policy favoring lawful marriage and legitimate offspring — and therefore unenforceable. The consortium contract is something like the marriage "contract" which makes plans for divorce, alimony, and so forth in the course of a happy marriage. The only time a contract contemplating divorce is enforceable in the courts is when it is a property settlement agreement made in the course of genuine hostilities, that is, in settlement of a divorce case *after* it has been filed. Both the marriage "contract" contemplating divorce and the consortium "contract" planning unmarriage are generally void and unenforceable because they are contrary to public policy which favors the institution of marriage.

With the understanding, then, that this "contract" is a "gentlemen's agreement" only, unenforceable in the courts, here is the general idea. Pick out the clauses you like, revise what you will and toss out the rest.

CONTRACT OF CONSORTIUM

This contract made and entered into this ____ day of _____, 19____, at _____, by and between _____ (hereinafter referred to as Consort I) and _____ (hereinafter referred to as Consort II); and

WHEREAS: Consort I and Consort II love each other; and

WHEREAS: the parties desire to share joint rents and phone bills, and to share the same dwelling; and

WHEREAS: the parties are having sexual relations and have decided to live openly together whatever their folks may think.

NOW, THEREFORE, in consideration of the hereinafter described covenants, the sufficiency of which as consideration are acknowledged by the parties, it is therefore agreed as follows:

1. The parties agree to be emotionally committed to each other and to love, honor, and respect each other until the first to occur of the following:

    A. until death do they part;

    B. until this agreement is substituted by lawful marriage between the parties;

    C. until either party decides to split.

2. The parties shall commence to live together on the ____ day of _____, 19____.

3. The parties have heretofore agreed that (strike the inapplicable clause):

    A. each is and shall remain employed on a full-time basis and each shall use best efforts to continue to be so employed;

    B. Consort ____ is and shall remain employed on a full-time basis and shall use (*his or her*) best efforts to continue to be so employed and Consort ____ is and shall remain unemployed (*or* employed on a part-time basis only).

4. The parties each agree to use their own names and in all respects to identify themselves as single people.

5. Neither party shall use the credit of the other.

6. Neither party shall claim alimony or rights in community property against the other.

7. Each party shall file and pay his or her own federal, state, and

local income taxes and each shall file returns for same as for a single person.

8. The parties agree that money shall be governed by the terms hereof.

    A. "Individual Funds": The parties acknowledge that each has his or her own savings, earnings, and other assets and each shall have the right to retain same separately, secretly, and in any form as to title and investment each chooses as to his or her own assets; and

    B. "Joint Funds System": Certain financial obligations, particularly as relate to the management of the consortium residence and hereinafter listed, shall be due and payable by each consort out of his or her own individual funds in his or her own separate bank accounts using the "joint funds system." The "joint funds system" works as follows: On the 15th day of April of each year of the consortium, the parties shall reveal to each other their respective annual incomes after taxes. Each party shall be entitled to deduct therefrom the following fixed liabilities:

        (1) alimony due and payable and actually paid to a prior spouse by reason of a court order;

        (2) child support due and payable and actually paid for the support of a child or children;

        (3) _____.

The net income figures thus arrived at shall be added together and a ratio achieved by dividing the total into Consort I's net income and achieving one percentage and then dividing the total into Consort II's net income and achieving the second percentage. All obligations hereinafter determined to be joint funds system obligations shall be payable promptly on the basis of that consort's percentage obligation. (For example, Consort I's net income after taxes and after above-listed deductions is $15,000. Consort II's net income after taxes and after above-listed deductions is $20,000. The total is $35,000. Divide $35,000 into Consort I's net income and the percentage achieved is 43 percent. Divide $35,000 into Consort II's net income and the percentage achieved is 57 percent. Let's say your rent is $400 a month and you've decided that rent is an item that should be paid under the "joint funds system." Consort I would pay 43 percent of the rent each month, being $172, and Consort II would pay 57 percent of the rent each month, being $228. The landlord therefore collects his $400 and neither consort is living above his or her means.)

The parties each acknowledge that unemployment and hard times are a possibility. Each agrees to be kind and understanding of the other's hard times and the suffering party acknowledges that he or she shall not unduly burden the employed party. The parties also understand that an unemployed consort who remains so by agreement of the other, under the terms of Paragraph 3 above, gets fully supported by the employed consort under the joint funds system formula.

C. "Equal Obligation System": Certain financial obligations shall be payable by the parties equally.

D. Nothing herein contained shall be construed as limiting the right of one consort to bestow gifts upon the other, and gifts once bestowed shall be the sole and exclusive property of the recipient.

9. All items for the use and benefit of only one consort shall be payable from "individual funds," including for example:

A. Clothes cleaning, cosmetics, beauty shop, barber shop, and other expenses incurred for personal grooming;

B. Medical and dental bills;

C. Business trips, business entertaining, and other business expenses;

D. Long distance telephone calls;

E. Clothes;

F. Investments (stocks, bonds, etc.);

G. Entertainment of one consort only.

(Strike Paragraph 9 if inapplicable by reason of a consort remaining unemployed under the terms of Paragraph 3 above and being without funds.)

10. The following items shall be payable promptly using the "joint funds system":

A. Rentals on the rented consortium residence;

    B. Utilities (excluding long distance telephone charges which shall be paid by the consort incurring same) incident to the use and occupancy of the consortium residence;

    C. Food and related grocery items and liquor purchased for consumption in the consortium residence (excluding items purchased for the purpose of entertaining the friends or family of only one consort, unless the other consort is in attendance at said function and there are leftovers for more than two full meals in which said other consort shares;

    D. Vacation trips taken by the consorts together;

    E. _____.

11. The following items shall be payable promptly using the "equal obligation system":

    A. Entertainment of both consorts together (such as theater tickets, dinner out, etc.);

    B. Gifts for mutual friends;

    C. _____.

12. The parties shall maintain a cookie jar for the purpose of depositing all receipts, bills, cash register tapes and evidence of payment of joint funds and equal obligation systems items, and the parties shall go through same at least monthly for the purpose of divvying up expenses on the basis of the joint funds system formula or the equal obligation system, whichever is applicable.

13. The parties shall each be responsible for the maintenance and cleanliness of the consortium residence equally or as nearly equally as possible (and especially scrubbing the bathroom), except that the following day-to-day tasks are assigned as follows:

Consort I:

Consort II:

14. (Strike if inapplicable.) The parties agree that they will employ a cleaning person ____ days each _____ and said person shall be paid from the joint funds system.

15. During the consortium the parties may elect to invest in stocks, bonds, or other such assets jointly by an equal investment of funds by the parties and said assets shall be held in joint tenancy with the right of survivorship. On termination of the consortium, the said assets shall be sold on the open market to the highest bidder for cash and the parties shall divide the proceeds equally.

16. The parties acknowledge that each has acquired prior to the time of occupancy of the consortium residence the following items of furniture, furnishings, housewares, and appliances:

Consort I:

Consort II:

On a termination of the consortium, each party shall retain as his or her own property each and every item set forth above as his or her own.

It is understood and agreed that from time to time the parties or either of them shall acquire additional items of furniture, furnishings, housewares, and appliances. On termination of the consortium each item purchased or acquired by gift by one consort shall be the sole and exclusive property of the consort. On termination, items purchased by or acquired by gift to the consortium shall be disposed of by passing title to the highest bidder for cash.

17. Notwithstanding anything herein contained to the contrary, if, under the terms of Paragraph 3 above, a consort remains unemployed or employed part-time for less than ＿＿＿ hours per week and has principal responsibility for the upkeep and maintenance of the consortium residence, and if the consortium continues in effect without interruption of for a period of ＿＿＿ years, then the employed consort acknowledges the prior services of the unemployed consort and shall be obligated to provide and maintain the following:

A. The employed consort shall name the unemployed consort his or her beneficiary for pension benefits if same are available; and

B. The employed consort shall provide life insurance on his or her life for the benefit of the unemployed consort in the minimum sum of $_____ in benefits, whether by naming the unemployed consort as beneficiary or by naming the employed consort's estate and preparing a will providing that the said amount shall be specifically bequeathed to the unemployed consort on the death of the employed consort; and

C. The employed consort shall pay a monthly support allowance subsequent to termination of the consortium to the unemployed consort in an amount equal to the actual food expense of the unemployed consort and one-half of the actual rent expense of the unemployed consort.

The obligations and benefits provided hereinabove shall remain in effect until the first to occur of the following:

A. Either consort dies; or

B. The unemployed consort marries or enters into another consortium; or

C. The unemployed consort becomes employed at an income greater than or equal to the income of the employed consort; or

D. The conclusion of _____ months for every year that the consortium remained in effect.

18. The parties shall reside at _____, in the City of _____, County of _____ and State of _____ (the "consortium residence").

19. The consortium residence shall be a (*rented apartment or home* or *owned cooperative or condominium apartment or home*). (Strike the inapplicable provision.)

20. (Paragraphs 20 to 23 relate to a *rented* consortium residence. Strike if inapplicable.)

The parties shall enter into a lease of _____ months' duration commencing the _____ day of _____, 19_____, each executing same in his or her own name. Each party shall have an equal right to the use and occupancy of said apartment until the first to occur of the following:

A. termination of the lease; or

B. termination of the consortium, at which time the provisions contained in Paragraphs 21, 22, or 23 hereof shall govern.

21. In the event the consortium terminates prior to the end of the lease term and neither consort wishes to remain in the consortium

residence, both shall be liable to each other to pay their share of rent under the joint funds system and each consort shall use his or her best efforts and cooperate with the other to sublet said consortium residence to a suitable sublessee acceptable to the landlord.

22. In the event the consortium terminates prior to the end of the lease and only one consort desires to remain on the premises, then the other consort shall vacate as soon as practicable and shall be liable to the other to continue to pay his or her share of the rent under the joint funds system until the first to occur of the following:

    A. the remaining consort's obtaining a replacement consort, roommate, or spouse; or

    B. the end of the lease term; or

    C. completion of a period of _____ months from the date of vacation of the premises by the vacating consort.

23. In the event the consortium terminates prior to the end of the lease term, and both consorts wish to remain in the consortium residence, then the consortium residence shall be the sole and exclusive residence of the consort who qualifies as hereinbelow:

    A. If the consortium has a child or children either born of both of the parties or adopted by both of them, then the consort with prime custody of the said offspring shall have the right to remain on the premises as his or her sole and exclusive residence. If this condition does not apply then subpart B shall govern.

    B. If the consortium residence was, prior to the consortium, the residence of one consort, then that consort shall have the right to remain on the premises as his or her sole and exclusive residence. If this condition does not apply then subpart C shall govern.

    C. If the consortium residence has been "materially improved" by the labor or money of one consort, then that consort shall have the right to remain on the premises as his or her exclusive residence. "Materially improved" means improved by work which is not practicably portable and which adds substantially to the value of the premises, including, for example, custom-made draperies, shutters for unusual windows, tacked-down carpeting, built-in carpentry, etc. If the parties cannot agree as to whether the premises were "materially improved," the definition of "capital improvement" contained in the Federal

Internal Revenue Code and as therein interpreted shall govern. If this condition does not apply, then subpart D shall govern.

D. If none of the above applies, then the parties shall either flip a coin and the winner, 2 out of 3, stays — or continue arguing until the end of the lease term and then both shall move.

The consort who vacates under the terms of this paragraph shall have no obligation whatever to the remaining consort for rents from the date of his or her vacation of the premises and the remaining consort shall pay all of the rent promptly as it is due until the end of their lease term and shall idemnify and hold the vacating consort harmless for any claims of the landlord.

24. (Paragraphs 24 to 27 relate to an *owned* consortium residence. Strike if inapplicable.)

The parties shall enter into a contract of purchase of the mutually agreed upon consortium residence.

The parties shall acquire same in joint tenancy with the right of survivorship (so that on the death of either party, title passes automatically to the other).

The parties shall make the down payment and the following payments: mortgage, assessment, real estate taxes, home owners' insurance, using the joint funds system.

Each party shall have an equal right to the use and occupancy of said owned consortium residence until the termination of the consortium, at which time the provisions contained in Paragraphs 25, 26, or 27 hereof shall govern.

25. In the event the consortium terminates and neither consort wishes to remain in the consortium residence, then the parties shall cooperate in placing same for sale immediately and using their best efforts to sell same, and upon a sale of the consortium residence the proceeds shall be divided equally (unless the consortium terminates within one year of the consorts' consummation of the purchase of the consortium residence, in which event the proceeds shall be divided in accordance with the ratio of actual cash contribution).

26. In the event the consortium terminates and only one consort desires to remain on the premises, then the other consort shall vacate as soon as practicable and shall have no further obligations to the remaining consort as to mortgage payments, assessment, or any other obligations in connection with the consortium residence from the date of vacation, and the remaining consort shall guarantee that all of said

obligations shall be paid promptly and indemnify the vacating consort and hold the vacating consort harmless on all of said obligations. The vacating consort shall execute and deliver quitclaim deed conveying all of his or her right, title, and interest in the consortium residence to the remaining consort and shall receive in exchange:

A. A written and legally enforceable guarantee of the mortgage and all other obligations and an indemnity in favor of the vacating consort executed by the remaining consort; and

B. A sum of money equal to the sum arrived at by the following computation:

(1) The parties shall add up the vacating consort's down payment and mortgage payments, principal and interest, real estate taxes, assessment, home owners' insurance payments and the like.

(2) That sum shall be divided by the number of months that the vacating consort actually occupied the consortium residence.

(3) The parties shall obtain, either by their own agreement, or by consulting with a professional in real estate management familiar with the area, the rent which would be charged on the open market if the consortium residence were rented instead of owned.

(4) The parties shall apply the joint funds system to ascertain what rent the vacating consort would have paid if the consortium residence were rented by the consorts at the rental arrived at under subpart 3 hereinabove for the period of actual occupancy and if the rent had been paid by the joint funds system.

(5) If the figure arrived at in subparts 1 and 2 hereinabove exceeds the amount arrived at in subparts 3 and 4 hereinabove, the remaining consort shall promptly pay the excess sum to the vacating consort. If the figure arrived at in subparts 1 and 2 hereinabove are less than the amount arrived at in subparts 3 and 4 hereinabove, then the vacating consort shall get a handshake only.

27. In the event the consortium terminates and both consorts wish to remain in the owned consortium residence, then the consortium residence shall be the sole and exclusive residence of the consort who qualifies hereinbelow:

A. If the consortium has a child or children either born of both of the parties or adopted by both of them, then the consort with prime custody of the said offspring shall have the right to remain on the premises as his or her sole and exclusive residence. If this condition does not apply then subpart B shall govern.

B. If the consortium residence was, prior to the consortium, the residence of one consort, then that consort shall have the right to remain on the premises as his or her sole and exclusive residence. If this condition does not apply then subpart C shall govern.

C. If the consortium residence has been "materially improved" by the labor or money of one consort, then that consort shall have the right to remain on the premises as his or her exclusive residence. "Materially improved" means improved by work which is not practicably portable and which adds substantially to the value of the premises, including, for example, custom-made draperies, shutters for unusual windows, tacked-down carpeting, built-in carpentry, etc. If the parties cannot agree as to whether premises were "materially improved," the definition of "capital improvement" contained in the Federal Internal Revenue Code and as thereunder interpreted shall govern. If this condition does not apply, then subpart D shall govern.

D. If none of the above applies, then the parties shall flip a coin and the winner, 3 out of 5, stays.

The consort who vacates shall have no further obligations to the remaining consort as to mortgage, assessment, or any other obligations in connection with the consortium residence from the date of vacation, and the remaining consort shall guarantee that all of said obligations shall be paid promptly and indemnify the vacating consort and hold the vacating consort harmless on all of said obligations. The vacating consort shall have the option either to

(1) Execute immediately a quitclaim deed to the remaining consort in exchange for the consideration arrived at under the formula set forth in paragraph 26 subpart B subparagraphs 1–5 above; or

(2) Continue on the title as joint tenant with the right of survi-

vorship with no further obligations until the first to occur of the following:

(a) death of either consort; or
(b) sale, at which time the proceeds of sale shall be divided equally between the consorts; or
(c) completion of a period _____ times the period the parties actually occupied the consortium residence together as consorts.

28. The parties agree to use birth control measures and their best efforts to avoid conception unless or until they jointly decide to have offspring. In the event that conception occurs in the absence of joint agreement to have children, then the provisions of Paragraph 29 shall apply. In the event that conception occurs by reason of joint agreement to have children, then the provisions of Paragraph 30 shall apply.

29. In the event that there is no agreement of the parties to have a child, then immediately upon one consort's ascertaining that she is pregnant, she is to divulge same to the other consort and the parties shall then promptly determine whether they are in agreement to have the child. If an agreement then occurs, the provisions of paragraph 30 will go into effect.

In the event the parties do not agree to have the child, then it shall be the sole and exclusive decision of the pregnant consort, with the advice of her physician, to either terminate the pregnancy by lawful abortion or to give birth to the baby and promptly release same for adoption. In the event of abortion or adoption all expenses directly related to same, including, for example, hospital bills, medical care, and drugs, not covered by insurance, shall be paid by the joint funds system.

In the event the pregnant consort determines to continue the pregnancy and keep the bastard, then the said directly related expenses not covered by insurance shall be paid out of the joint funds system. In the event of a pregnancy and birth unconsented to by the father, then on termination of the consortium, custody and support shall be as follows:

A. The mother shall have the right to be the prime custodian of the bastard, with reasonable visitation rights in the father; and
B. The noncustodial parent's obligation of support shall be limited to the actual total cost of food for the bastard and the actual cost of babysitting and day care for the bastard, which

sums shall be paid monthly until the bastard is emancipated.*
All other expenses shall be the sole and exclusive obligation of
the custodial parent; and

C. The parents shall pay for extraordinary medical and dental
expenses of the bastard on the joint funds system. The phrase
extraordinary medical and dental expenses shall include the
treatment of grave and serious illness or emergency and excludes orthodontia. The custodial parent shall, except in emergency when time in treatment is essential, consult in advance
with the noncustodial parent as to extraordinary medical and
dental expenses to be incurred in the treatment of the bastard.

D. The noncustodial parent's obligations set forth in subparts B
and C above shall be multiplied by the number of unagreed-
to bastards born to the parties.

30. In the event the parties agree to have a child, then all expenses
directly related to pregnancy and delivery, including, for example,
hospital bills, medical care, and drugs, not covered by insurance, shall
be paid by the joint funds system. The mother may, at her option, take
a leave of absence from employment or terminate same, and if she does
so and is without salary by reason of same, the father shall be obligated
to provide for her reasonable support at a standard in conformance
with the circumstances previously enjoyed by the parties for the period of said unemployment, but in no event to exceed ____ months. On
termination of the consortium, custody and support shall be as follows:

A. In the event that the bastard is breast-fed, then during the
term of breast-feeding, the mother shall be the prime custodian of the bastard with reasonable visitation rights in the
father; and

B. In all other events, prime custody shall be in the party desirous
of same, and if the consorts cannot agree who shall have prime
custody then prime custody shall be in the consort who shall
serve the best interest of the bastard, and standards of same
are:

(1) love and affection;

* The term "emancipated" means the bastard's becoming of legal age, or marrying, or obtaining full-time employment, or undertaking a residence apart
from both parents — whichever is first to occur.

(2) responsibility;

(3) quantity of time devoted exclusively to the bastard;

(4) experience with infants and children;

(5) patience;

(6) stability;

(7) _____.

C. It is understood and agreed that the parties recognize that it is in the best interests of the bastard to have a stable and unified environment and not to be bounced from parent to parent, and that siblings whether half-siblings or whole siblings should remain together where possible.

D. The noncustodial parent's obligation of support shall be limited to the actual total cost of food for the bastard, clothing for the bastard, babysitting and day care for the bastard and one-quarter of the rent or monthly mortgage payment actually incurred by the custodial parent, which sums shall be paid monthly until the bastard is emancipated; and

E. The parents shall pay for extraordinary medical and dental expenses of the bastard on the joint funds system. The phrase extraordinary medical and dental expenses shall include the treatment of grave and serious illness or emergency, and includes orthodontia. The custodial parent shall, except in emergency when time in treatment is essential, consult in advance with the noncustodial parent as to extraordinary medical and dental expenses to be incurred in the treatment of the bastard.

F. The noncustodial parent's obligations set forth in subparts D and E above shall be multiplied by the number of bastards born by agreement of the parties but in no event shall the rental or mortgage expense due from the noncustodial parent exceed one-half of the actual obligation (except during the period covered in Paragraph 30, line 9 above).

31. Notwithstanding any of the provisions contained in Paragraphs 28 to 30 hereinabove, the parties expressly agree:

A. The bastard shall have the surname of _____; and

B. Both parties will at all times notify each other as to his and her whereabouts from the date of obtaining knowledge of pregnancy to the date of the emancipation of the bastard; and

C. Both parties will take whatever legal steps are necessary in his or her domiciliary state to acknowledge the bastard as his and her own, but in no event shall this clause be construed to require the parties to marry; and

D. The custodial parent shall not surrender custody of the bastard to any third person either during his or her life or by will without giving the noncustodial parent prior actual personal notice at the last address provided and the right to accept custody of the bastard before the bastard is turned over to a third person, nor shall either parent surrender the bastard for adoption without actual personal notice to the other parent at the last address provided and the right of the other parent to accept custody; and

E. Both parties shall use their best efforts to provide the bastard with material comforts, medical care, and education commensurate with their ability so to do over and above the requirements of support applicable under the support provisions contained in this agreement; and

F. Both parties shall use their best efforts to provide life insurance on their lives for the benefit of the bastard until the bastard is emancipated in the minimum sum of $_____ of benefits.

32. In the event that either party is an alien and is denied naturalization or is charged in deportation proceedings by reason of the consortium relationship or sexual conduct between the consorts, then all legal fees, expenses, and costs shall be payable promptly under the joint funds system.

33. In the event that either party is terminated from employment by reason of the consortium relationship or sexual conduct between consorts, or pregnancy by reason of sexual intercourse between consorts, then all legal fees, expenses, and costs directed toward seeking reinstatement shall be payable promptly under the joint funds system and if said efforts should be successful and back pay or other funds are ordered paid and actually paid, then the consort receiving same shall pay to the other an amount equal to the lesser of one-half of the amount received or the other consort's share of legal fees, costs, and expenses.

34. In the event that either party is charged with violating any criminal law by reason of the consortium relationship or sexual conduct between the consorts, then all legal fees, expenses, and costs shall be payable promptly under the joint funds system and each consort

agrees to visit the other during any period of incarceration and give him or her aid, comfort, cigarettes, and a chess set.

35. The parties agree that each shall make a valid will, revocable on termination of the consortium, providing that a like percentage share of their respective estates shall pass on death to the other.

36. This agreement is severable so that if any of it is enforceable, each enforceable part shall be enforced notwithstanding that any or all other parts are thrown right out of court.

37. This agreement shall be construed by the laws of the State of _____, and if that state won't enforce it, then by the laws of any other state or states of the United States that will.

IN WITNESS WHEREOF, with serious doubts as to the enforceability of the above, but in good faith and intending to carry out the provisions hereof whether or not a court orders them to do so, the parties hereto set forth their respective hands and seals, at the date set forth above at the City of _____, State of _____.

_____ (Seal)

Consort I

_____ (Seal)

Consort II

Noting that their hands are trembling and that both are considering the sanctity of marriage and the relative security of divorce laws, but facing this brave new lifestyle with chins up, _____ (Consort I) and _____ (Consort II) executed this "contract" in our presence this ____ day of _____, 19____.

_____

Witness

_____

Witness

INDEX